Around the

Around the World in a Kilt

John B McMillan

SWEETSPIRE LITERATURE
—— MANAGEMENT ——

Table of Contents

CHAPTER 1

Icebreaker

Migrating South

Having checked in at Inverness Airport, I passed through security to the departure lounge. A man detached himself from his group of friends and approached me.

"Excuse me sir, would you allow me to have a photograph taken with you?" He was with a group of Spaniards who'd been holidaying in the Scottish highlands. He passed his camera to one of his friends, posed with me for a few shots, and thanked me. Airport lounges are good places for people-watching, but that day every eye seemed to be watching *me*. I was wearing my kilt.

I had been wearing it a lot since I had returned from my previous round the world trip in the spring of that year. It is easier to get into a kilt than a pair of trousers when your leg is encased in a plaster cast from top to toe, the result of having broken my Achilles Tendon while travelling in Fiji. That had forced me to abort my previous trip a few weeks earlier than intended to come home for surgery, but here I was again, like a bird about to migrate southwards at the start of October.

On my previous trip around the world I had travelled light. When I had checked in at Inverness Airport and the clerk told me to weigh my baggage, I laid my weekend backpack on the weighing machine.

"Put all your luggage on," she said.

"That *is* all my luggage."

She looked again at my ticket, flicked through the several pages of it. "But you're going round the world for six months - and that small bag is all you are taking?"

"You don't need much clothing in the tropics," I replied.

But on this trip, warm clothing was going to be essential to combat the cold, wet weather likely to be encountered among the Patagonian Mountains. And you need more than shorts and flip-flops when tramping across the snow and ice of Antarctica, the coldest place on earth.

On my first visit to the Cook Islands, I had regretted my decision not to bring my kilt. The Cook Islanders' respect for ancestry, their desire to retain their traditions in music and dance, and the effort they put into making traditional costumes left me feeling I had betrayed my own culture. The kilt, recognised throughout the world as a Scottish icon, attracts attention and arouses curiosity.

While wearing my kilt, I have been approached by admiring strangers who called me sexy, cute, handsome, manly - and who am I to disagree? That never happens when I wear trousers!

On my previous trip I had reasoned that, as most of the travelling would be in the tropics, it would be too warm to wear the kilt. Big mistake! Air conditioning in planes and airports can be cool, so wearing the kilt while travelling is quite comfortable. Better still, it attracts the attention of sweet flight attendants who offer me extra goodies as I walk about the plane for exercise on long-haul flights. They even drag me into their kitchen area for conversation. It is amazing how many people in the world have a Scottish granny! It can be too hot to wear the kilt during the day in the tropics, other than for a short time; but to dress up for a night out, it's fine and enhances the experience.

The kilt adds another dimension to travel. The evidence was there at Inverness before I had even left my homeland. It is a good way to meet people and make friends. And it proved to be a key that opened the door of opportunity and led to all sorts of interesting situations...

At Motueka, New Zealand, I was striding along the main street, kilt swinging, when a lady emerged from a shop. Her eyes, and her arms, opened wide and without a word of introduction, she wrapped herself around me and hugged me. I had been told New Zealanders were friendly, but this was overwhelming.

"You must be from Scotland," she murmured, holding me close.

"How did you know that?" I mocked, my lips caressing the lobe of her ear.

"I love men in kilts. My grandmother was a MacPherson," she murmured, still holding me close.

"My great-grandmother was a MacPherson," I said.

She leaned back, still clinging to me. Her eyes opened wide again, "We are related!" And she gave me another lingering, body-clutching hug.

I said, "This is nice. Tell me the names of some of your other ancestors. Maybe we're related some more."

She released me from her clutches and looked me straight in the eye. "*You* are coming home with me for lunch." My pulse quickened. Then she spoiled it: "My husband will be delighted to meet you."

I couldn't complain though. She served up a delicious seafood lunch, with stirring pipe-band music playing in the background. It was a warm welcome to New Zealand, but it would never have happened had I not been wearing the kilt.

There are the inevitable requests for information, usually from ladies, about what is worn under the kilt, to which the standard response is: "Madam, nothing is *worn* under the kilt - *it is all in fine working order*!" It does become a bit tiresome though. Just imagine the reaction if men started asking every woman who wore a skirt if she was wearing knickers. The cry of 'pervert' would resound around the world. Yet it's regarded as acceptable for a woman to make such personal enquiries of a man in the kilt. Come on girls, play fair.

Another interesting encounter happened in New Zealand when I went into a pub which advertised: Three Course Meals - Choice of Roasts - as much as you can eat for $12. Well, that's not the kind of bargain a hungry Scotsman could ignore. I joined the queue.

I noticed two women gazing at me, their heads close together as they discussed my attire. As I rejoined the queue for dessert, one of the women rose and sidled up close behind me. Really close. I could feel her hot breath on my ear as she panted, "Go on, let's see what's under your kilt."

Maybe I'm old-fashioned, but I thought that was a bit forward. "I'm flattered by your interest, but how would you feel if I came up behind you and asked to see what was under your skirt?"

"Oh, that's no problem." She lifted up the front of her skirt to reveal a fine pair of strapping thighs and rather saucy underwear - I couldn't help noticing! "Right, I've done my bit. Now it's your turn," she said.

I had to think fast. "Och, haud oan the noo, hen. (I think better in the vernacular). You can do that because you're wearing something under your skirt, but if I lifted my kilt I could be arrested for indecent exposure."

"You're kidding."

"Why ask, if you won't believe me?"

"So, it's true then?"

"You're looking at the genuine article here."

She eyed me up and down lasciviously and said, "Well, if it takes a skirt that long to cover it, you must be one hell of a guy!"

CHAPTER 2

Adrift

MV Taka

One of the most disconcerting sights for a diver is to reach the surface after a dive, look around for the dive-boat, and find an empty ocean. That is a true test of your ability to control panic.

At the start of my live-aboard dive trip off the coast of Queensland on board the dive boat, Taka, the ship's divemaster had briefed us on the safety procedures, insisting that we must sign our names on the dive sheet when we went off the boat, and when we came back aboard after a dive. It was forbidden to have someone else do it for us. He emphasised the importance of this by telling us of an Australian dive boat that had been casual about such matters and returned to Cairns, leaving a couple of divers still underwater. They have never been seen since. That event inspired the film, Open Water, which attempted to describe the probable outcome - and it was not cheerful viewing.

When I broke the surface that day with my dive buddy, *our* ship was nowhere to be seen either - and we were 200 miles from Australia, out in the Pacific Ocean. Unlike in the film, we didn't see any black fins circling around us - yet - but in the dive briefing before we left the ship, we had been warned to stay close to the reef as the tidal currents whipping round a nearby corner were very strong and could carry us out to the depths where tiger sharks, one of the few species that might attack a human, were known to patrol.

To avoid being swept away in the current on entering the water, we had to grab a floating rope attached to the mooring buoy and use it to pull ourselves against the current to the buoy. Clinging to its anchor line, we could then descend, hand over hand, to a shelf at 18 metres depth. Once there we would be sheltered from the strength of the current by the reef and could explore it as we wished. Simple. Aye, right! As Robert Burns, Scotland's national poet, once wrote: *The best laid schemes o' mice and men gang aft agley.*

On reaching the mooring buoy, I signalled to Eric, my Australian dive buddy, that I was ready to descend. He returned the signal. I released air from my buoyancy vest, slipped below the waves, and made my way down the mooring line. When I could see the seabed below me, I looked back to check that Eric was following. He wasn't. I arrested my descent.

Still at the surface, he was struggling with his buoyancy. Sometimes the buoyancy vest traps a pocket of air and you need to angle one shoulder down to get a vertical run to let all the air out the valve. I made my way back up to help. That's the role of the buddy, stay close to your partner and give assistance when required. Using my negative buoyancy to lower his right shoulder, we got him tilted and some air hissed out. I slipped below the surface and worked my way down the rope again. But he was still having trouble getting down. I ascended again. He was fiddling with his buoyancy apparatus at about three metres depth. I released my grip on the mooring line to check all his air was out, but he let go too and the strong current took us both towards the stern of the ship, now visible above us. I indicated that we should swim for the reef.

We angled ourselves across the current and finned our way towards the reef. At least, that's what we appeared to be doing. Visibility was not good and the ship had disappeared from view. There was no sign of either the shelf below, or the reef ahead of us. Still, we headed in the right direction, descending all the time. A deepening blue void enveloped us. I checked my dive computer: 17 metres. The shelf should be right below us. But it wasn't. It was time to neutralise buoyancy to stop descending, level out, and find the reef. We swam harder in the direction of the reef hoping that we would pick up sight of it, or the shelf, at any moment.

But we didn't.

With startling suddenness, a flash of light pierced the blue gloom. It glowed for a few seconds and then dimmed. It was followed by another, and another, and yet more. They were all around us: beautiful lights flashing like sapphires. It was like floating in space among the stars. Their beauty was indescribable. I wanted the whole world to see this. I had found paradise down here in the depths of the ocean. I could die quite happily here.

I could imagine choirs of angels singing serene harmonies to accompany the wondrous sights around me as I made my euphoric way towards the gates of heaven.

Something triggered in my brain and jolted me out of my euphoria. These illuminations were light emitting plankton; creatures which, when agitated, emit flashes of light. But these weren't the tiny, almost microscopic, dinoflagellates I have seen so often when sailing at night in Scotland. These flashes were much bigger; and so brilliant was the intensity of light they projected. Realisation hit me. Light emitting plankton of that size tend to be found in deep water.

Two words flashed into my mind: Nitrogen Narcossis. At depth, the nitrogen levels in the blood build up and can induce a feeling of euphoria. People become irrational in this condition and often do silly things, like taking their regulators out. I wondered how it was affecting Eric. Would he go crazy and go carousing off into the depths, and how would I get him up if he did? I wasn't a kick on the backside away from it already with my thoughts of pearly gates, and choirs of angels, and dying in a sea full of sapphires. There was no time to waste.

I checked my dive computer. The figures were flashing rapidly now: 34 metres, 35 metres, 36 metres. We should have touched the shelf at no more than 18 metres. The current, flowing off the shelf, had swept us out and down, like being carried over a waterfall, and we had missed the shelf completely. Our buoyancy was now decreasing as the tiny air pockets in our wet suits were compressed by the increase in pressure, and with the strong downward current we were accelerating towards the floor of the ocean 1,000 metres below.

I reached out and touched Eric, pointed to the dive computer on my wrist and signalled to ascend. He checked his computer and signalled his agreement. We pumped air from our tanks into our vests to counteract the strength of the downward pull and began to rise once more. The beautiful lights died out. We kept on climbing, at a slow rate. Too fast a rate of ascent could cause an attack of the bends, a potentially fatal condition. We hovered at 5 metres for a three-minute decompression safety stop, then eased ourselves back to the surface and looked around. Taka was nowhere in sight.

Reason kicked in. It couldn't have left the area, because this was the first dive of the day and we had only been in the water about 15 minutes. The sea was lively, with a fresh breeze whipping up the waves, obscuring our view of the horizon. Our eyes were virtually at sea level and the sea was throwing up short, steep waves about a metre high. These must be preventing us from seeing the ship. I pumped more air into my buoyancy vest to raise me further out of the water and kicked hard with my fins to gain extra height, driving my body up till my waistline was about level with the surface, turning a full circle as I did so. As I crested a wave, the ship came into view a long way off. Although we had been swimming hard towards the reef, we had been swept in the opposite direction by the current and were about half a mile away from where we should have been.

"It's over there. Let's swim for it." I called to Eric. But the current was too strong. We were being driven still further away. The divemaster's warning came into mind: we were now in the territory of the tiger sharks. That wasn't a very comforting thought. I looked around. No fins - and this was no time for such thoughts either.

The mathematician in me took control. Considering the enormous expanse of the Pacific Ocean, the probability that there were tiger sharks in the vicinity seemed slight, let's say a 1-in-1000 chance. And if one would be aggressive enough to have a nibble at us? Most don't. Let's say also 1-in-1000. Then the probability of our being attacked by a shark was a million to one in our favour. That was a more comforting thought. Like eating porridge, or a portion of green vegetables, a knowledge of mathematics is a healthy thing. It is good for controlling panic. I hoped Eric hadn't been thinking of the sharks, and that my estimate of the probabilities was reasonable.

I called out to him. "It's a waste of time swimming. Let's inflate the sausages." These are sausage-shaped surface marker buoys. When filled with air they rise erect from the sea and the bright orange colour attracts the attention of the lookouts posted on the dive boat.

That's the theory anyway.

All the other divers should be surfacing ahead of the boat, going up the mooring line, but we were a long way astern. I hoped the lookouts on the ship would be scanning the sea all round, just in case. We filled the sausages with air from our tanks and blew our whistles in the hope of attracting attention. I wondered if sharks could hear. I have since learned they can.

There we were, lying on our backs holding what looked like enormous condoms sticking up in the air. Again to make light of things I called out, "Hey, Eric! It's the first time I've had a 2 metre erection." He grinned. It worked and helped ease away the fears. He confessed to me later that he was really concerned at that point and making light of the situation was the best medicine.

A few moments later, we saw the ship's boat pull away from the stern and turn towards us. It was soon alongside, heaved us each a line with a handle on the end, and towed us, like a couple of logs, back to the ship. The divemaster was waiting. He checked us back aboard on the dive list - and then we had some explaining to do.

I told him about the problem with Eric's buoyancy, and in attempting to solve the problem we had floated free of the mooring line when Eric had let go. Big mistake. At least one hand should have been kept on the line. The current did the rest. But after that point we'd done all we'd been trained to do. We stayed close together. We kept in constant communication. If we had been affected by nitrogen narcosis, we still were 'compos mentis' enough to make a proper, safe ascent. We'd tried to swim back, but on realising we couldn't we'd deployed the safety signal. The crew of the boat were keeping proper watch and we were picked up. The training, the teamwork, and the vigilance of the look-outs had been effective. He studied me for a moment to let all this sink in, nodded his head and said, "Yeah. You're right." Then he turned to Eric: "But what was the problem with your buoyancy?"

Eric looked a bit sheepish. He'd felt cold in the water the day before and decided to put on an extra 3 millimetre wet suit. A wet suit adds a layer of tiny air bubbles, increasing his buoyancy. He should also have added extra lead weights to his belt to counteract that increase. But he'd forgotten. He looked at me, shamefaced, and began to apologise.

I reassured him. "Och, anybody can make a mistake. The important thing is that we stuck together and remained a team throughout. It was a learning experience neither of us will forget!"

CHAPTER 3

Sharks Galore

That memorable dive occurred during the live-aboard trip I had planned to take the previous year, but had to cancel to return home for surgery to repair the Achilles Tendon I had broken in Fiji. After flying from Scotland via London and Singapore to Australia, I was met on arrival at Cairns by my friends, Bruce and Shirley Barrett, the parents of one of my outstanding pupils when I was teaching in an army school in Germany. I had enjoyed their hospitality on my last visit and they had insisted that I should stay with them again. On arrival, Shirley suggested I take an afternoon nap and a few hours later the delicious smell of a barbecue drifted through my bedroom window and brought me to my senses again. Next day, Bruce dropped me off at the youth hostel in town, from where the dive company's minibus took me to the docks.

Taka was a purpose-built dive boat specialising in trips to the most pristine parts of the Great Barrier Reef, and to Osprey Reef, some 200 miles east of Australia in the vastness of the Pacific Ocean. We steamed northwards overnight for about 250 miles, arriving at our first destination around 11 a.m. On our approach to the reef, my attention was caught by a splash in the sea ahead of us. A dark body and fin broke the surface in a characteristic leap.

Dolphins

"Dolphin ahead!" I shouted.

Everyone rushed to the bow. In the clear water we could see them jostling for the best position in the pressure wave ahead of the bow, like surfers, but underwater. A delight to watch, they stayed with us for about twenty minutes. It was an uplifting start to the day.

This part of the reef was well beyond the range of most of the boats operating out of Cairns. Further north than any other settlement along that coast, the reef had not suffered the same damage as many parts closer to areas of human habitation. Later in the day, we were to see the feeding of giant groupers, sometimes called potato cod, a fish around 5 feet long with a body as thick as a human torso. Discovering one resting under a coral overhang, I signalled to my dive buddy, Eric, to come and have a look. The huge fish gazed at him with as much curiosity as he gazed upon it.

It began to move towards him. Eric backed off. The fish still came forward, its face no more than about 30 centimetres from his. Its jaws seemed big enough to swallow his head. There was no hint of aggressiveness in its behaviour: with its huge pouting lips and big eyes looking into his, it seemed to have fallen in love with him. Eric confirmed later that he had been thinking along the same lines and was beginning to feel nervous in case its amorous looks were a prelude to an attempt at procreation.

Amorous Grouper

The divers sat in a circle on a sandy seabed to watch lunch being served to the fish. The divemaster took a bucket of food into the centre. A giant cod swam up to him and, with remarkable gentleness, took the morsel he offered. It then moved away, allowing another leviathan to come in for a serving. Swimming between the divers, these enormous fish caressed themselves against our bodies. I am not comfortable with the idea of feeding the fish. I believe you should affect their behaviour as little as possible, but it was an interesting diversion.

We did four dives each day, the last one a night dive. With a limited range of vision at night, only that illuminated by the torch beam, it is interesting how you begin to notice all sorts of small details of reef life that you tend to miss during the day. Tiny shrimps, their orange eyes like gemstones reflecting the beam of the torch, flit among the staghorn corals and when you get close they propel themselves backwards with a flick of the tail and the velocity of a bullet. Large lobsters (strictly speaking they are crayfish and lack the large crusher claws of the lobsters found in the North Atlantic) leave their rocky cavities and move about on the ocean floor in search of food.

During the day, visibility was around 40 metres: at night you see only a few metres ahead in the beam of your torch. What is lurking in the gloomy darkness beyond, you do not know. As I rose above a coral wall, I found myself face-to-face with a large shark. It was as surprised as I was, but it didn't like the look of me at all and, with a flick of its tail, it veered off to be consumed by the darkness. Large trevally hunt at night and will swim alongside you as they await your torch beam picking out small fish. With the small fish dazzled by the light, the trevally dive upon them from the shadows beside you with lightning rapidity. We tried to reduce the unfair advantage by not keeping the beam of light on small fish for too long: a limit of three hits per diver had been advised by the divemaster.

That night, the ship got under way to steam 200 miles out to Osprey Reef, a coral crust formed around the crater of an ancient submerged volcano. This reef is outstanding for the quality of coral and the diversity of marine life it supports. It is home to hundreds of different species of fish, many clothed in the most brilliant colours.

We explored a 'garden' of giant clams, their jaws a metre wide, coloured with abstract patterned membranes covering the gap between the two huge corrugated shells. We spiralled around coral pinnacles rising thirty metres from the shelf, festooned with multi-coloured growths, and explored reef walls fissured with dark caves and canyons, one of which had trapped an old anchor estimated to have been abandoned there around 150 to 200 years ago.

Giant Clam

On Steve's Bommie, a coral knoll, a memorial plaque had been placed about 18 metres down to commemorate a guy called Steve who loved free diving (diving without breathing apparatus). Well, poor Steve overdid it on one occasion and blacked out underwater, doing what he loved doing, but would never do again, and his friends placed this plaque on one of his favourite spots on this remote reef, 200 miles out in the ocean. It is not the kind of thing you expect to find at the bottom of the sea and it had a certain poignancy about it.

It was here we saw sharks being fed. The divers again were organised in a circle, perched on the bottom. Fish, recognising this gathering as the prelude to a feast, swam around in great numbers as we waited for the boat with the food to arrive. I was intrigued: hundreds of fish of all sizes migrated towards us, as though a signal had been beamed out over the reef. On my way down I saw a couple of sharks, but by the time everyone had assembled, no fewer than fifty sharks were circling above us, like aircraft waiting permission to land, mingling with hundreds of smaller fish, some giant groupers, and a passing turtle.

Grey Reef shark

The feast consisted of several large tuna heads with holes drilled in them and a chain threaded through to form a giant tuna-head kebab. The ship's boat arrived above and lowered the chain into the sea. The effect was electrifying. Sharks dived on it from all angles, tearing at the fish heads, shaking them from side to side like a terrier playing with a rag doll. Huge groupers barged in, their snouts butting sharks sideways to get at the food. Opportunist red snappers snatched at fragments of fish flying from the rips and tears of the sharks, and shot out again before being crushed among the bodies of the big fish. From this melee of writhing fish and snapping, tearing jaws, a shower of smaller fragments sprayed around like snowflakes for the little fish to snap up - crumbs from the big boys' table. It was mesmerising.

In the middle of this melee was Paul, our fearless crew cameraman, filming the action close up with his video camera and Ty, the divemaster, taking still pictures for the record of our voyage. As the frenzy began to subside and there were only a few fragments left, a huge moray eel raised its head from a hole in the coral just below the boys with the cameras and hooked its teeth into the last fish head. With its tail anchored in its hole in the coral, it then retreated, trying to pull the tuna head in with it, but the hole was not big enough and the head jammed at the entrance. Tugging at it seemed to excite the sharks once more and two or three dived upon it in another frenzy, tearing it away from the eel, and another round of shaking, wriggling, and snapping followed.

After that, we explored the reef. On sandy beds under ledges in the coral wall lay several hyperventilating sharks, exhausted by their efforts. They needed a post-prandial nap.

White-tipped reef shark

Many people express concern about the danger of swimming in waters populated by sharks, but let's put it in perspective. Compare a coconut with a shark. Which is more scary? Yet it is a fact that far more people are killed every year by falling coconuts than are attacked, let alone killed, by sharks. Only a few species of shark are capable of biting a human limb. Many of them have jaws designed for eating in other ways: sifting through coral sand for small crustaceans, or filtering plankton from the sea. Human limbs neither attract, nor are able to be eaten, by such mouths. We don't go around chewing up trees because our jaws are not up to the task, nor are our digestive systems capable of digesting wood. It's the same with sharks. Biting a human would be inconceivable for most of them. Sharks don't go around looking for people to eat for dinner. Humans are aliens in the marine environment and have never been an item in the food chain.

On average, around four or five shark attacks per year occur worldwide, when an occasional great white, or a tiger shark, may snap at arms or legs when they confuse swimmers with seals. Usually they spit the bits out. More often the victim dies through loss of blood, not by being eaten. Forget the sensationalist stories portrayed by films like 'Jaws.' Sharks are beautiful animals.

CHAPTER 4

Close to Home

O f all the countries I have visited, New Zealand is the one that most resembles my native Scotland. The South Island, with its rugged mountains fissured by deep inlets of the sea, sheep grazing on rounded hills, its forests and friendly people, generated an uncanny feeling that I was back at home.

I had flown into Christchurch at the insistence of Catriona Campbell, the daughter of my former doctor and friend, Stewart Campbell. Catriona had been a pupil at Alness Academy when I had been Assistant Head there. Now working in New Zealand as a nurse, and painting pictures in her spare time, she picked me up at the airport and I bunked down in her art studio.

On the first day, she took me to the harbour at Lyttleton, an almost land-locked natural harbour enclosed by rounded hills. It reminded me of the Cromarty Firth in the north of Scotland, where I had lived and worked for a number of years. The harbour and its ships often provided inspiration for Catriona's paintings, one of which now hangs on my wall.

To my surprise, tied up to the quay was the steam tug, Lyttleton, built in Scotland by Ferguson Brothers of Port Glasgow in 1907. Originally named Canterbury, it was re-named after Lyttleton harbour acquired a dredger named Canterbury. The Lyttleton was built in an era when the term 'Clyde-built' was synonymous with excellence, durability, and innovation in shipbuilding. The proof is there, for after more than a century this venerable lady is still operational, offering trips around the bay.

The tug Lyttleton

That brought back memories of my boyhood, sailing on the many pleasure steamers that had cruised the Firth of Clyde in summer. On those trips, a visit to the engine room of the ship was an obligatory part of the experience, and I soon found my way into the engine room on Lyttleton where an elderly Scottish engineer sat among the tangle of polished pipes, valves, pressure gauges, and oily pistons, all in fine working order thanks to the quality of materials, design, and the loving care of its engineers for more than a century.

It used to be said that on almost every ship in the world you would find a Scottish engineer - and this was no exception. (Fans of the futuristic film Star Trek will remember 'Scotty,' the Scottish chief engineer, maintaining that tradition). Despite having lived in

New Zealand since 1952, Lyttleton's engineer had lost none of his Clydeside accent. He looked a fair bit older than me, so I offered my assistance as stoker, shovelling coal into its hungry boiler to keep the steam pressure up - another new experience for me - and I loved every minute of it.

While Catriona drove me around the neighbourhood in her car, she asked if I would mind sharing her company at dinner one evening with a young man who had been paying some attention to her. Afterwards, when he had left, she said to me, "Can I ask you for an opinion, John? Not having my parents here, or knowing anyone from an older, more experienced generation that I can confide in, I felt that perhaps you could offer me an opinion on whether you think he is suitable boyfriend material."

I chuckled. "I am touched by your faith in me. He seems like a genuine guy to me: bright, intelligent, with a promising future ahead of him. Based on that short acquaintance, my gut feeling is positive - and that is a good sign. I see no reason to advise against exploring a friendship with him."

"But will you let me snog him?"

"Why not, if you like him? But keep your emotions under control!"

She chuckled. "Thanks John. I knew I could trust you to give me good advice."

Next day, Catriona dropped me off at the bus station for the long journey south to Queenstown, a spectacular mountain location in the South Island. I was now travelling solo, but getting round New Zealand is easy. Every hostel seems to have a travel desk offering loads of options from day-trips to month-long excursions. Go to the travel desk, pick your next destination or activity, and make the booking. A minibus will pick you up and take you to the bus station, your chosen activity, or all the way to your next location. Travelling at budget prices, you can gather information about places of interest from the other people sharing the minibus with you, and you never have to make a plan until each day dawns. Bungee jumping, high-speed rubber boat trips through canyons, sky-diving, kayaking, glacier hiking....its all there for the adrenalin junkies.

Queenstown has a small airfield and offers flights to and from Milford Sound, a spectacular fiord in the south west of the island. There is also a daily bus. I decided to go by bus and return by light aircraft. The route by bus took me through some mountain tunnels with signs advising: Do Not Enter In The Event Of An Earthquake. That seemed to make sense, but earthquakes don't give you a warning signal. What if you were inside the tunnel when an earthquake starts? Such thoughts had to be banished from my mind.

Milford Sound and the floating hostel

The scenery at Milford Sound was outstanding. I had booked into a floating hostel, a ship that took us to various parts of the fiord and carried some kayaks as well. Having owned a sea-going kayak in my youth in Scotland, I had to get afloat again. I love the intimacy with sea and shore that kayaking offers. It is almost silent and presents the human form in a different shape which enables you to get closer to wild life than would otherwise be possible. Gliding along in such a superb scenic location was a highlight of my tour.

The flight back in a small aircraft offered more thrills than I expected. The runway faced a steep rock face, so when the plane took off it had to make a sharp turn, with the rock face perilously near. On reaching cruising height, a deep valley lay around 2000 feet below us on one side, while a sheer rock face towered above us so close on the other side I felt I could almost reach out and touch it. Visibility was excellent the whole time, offering superb views of the mountains and the wide valley with Queenstown and its large lake as we approached. Though only a short flight, it had been worth every penny.

The following day, I was on the road again to do some glacier hiking - in my kilt - at the Franz Josef glacier on the South Island's west coast, another event that raised a lot of interest. You don't see many kilts crossing glaciers, or crawling through crevasses. I felt a bit uneasy about that, knowing that glaciers make their way at a slow pace down the mountain, and crevasses could close up. I didn't fancy being squeezed within a mass of ice for the next few thousand years, but our guide assured us that the situation was monitored each morning so the guides knew which crevasses were opening up and which were becoming tighter.

The rest of that day was spent kayaking on a tranquil lake. Wearing my kilt that evening, a young man at the hostel came over and asked which part of Scotland I was from.

"Och, you'll probably never have heard of it. It's a wee village called Lochcarron in the northwest highlands."

"Oh, I know it well," he said. "I did a mountaineering course there with Martin Moran." Martin was an outstanding mountaineer with many 'first ascents' to his name. He ran mountaineering courses in Scotland, as well as leading expeditions to Norway, the Alps, and the Nanda Devi region of the Himalayas, where he was killed in an avalanche in May 2019 during the attempted ascent of an un-climbed and un-named mountain. His body has never been found.

Browsing the tourist information and wondering where to stop next, I spotted a leaflet advertising the Hokitika Wild Food Festival. That sounded interesting. I booked a seat in the north-bound minibus the following morning and sitting beside me was a 17 year-old Dutch girl, backpacking her way solo around the world. She had no fear of travelling alone, preferred it in fact, an attitude I found in harmony with my own. Travelling solo makes decision making easier: you have the freedom to go where you please, when you please, and you are likely to meet more people and make friends by travelling alone. Travelling with friends can be a strain - I knew of one engaged couple who went their separate ways after the first 12,000 miles.

My young Dutch friend had done many things, including sky-diving.

"I have often thought of doing that," I said.

"Well, there are plenty of places in New Zealand offering it, so why don't you just go and do it the next time you see a sign offering it?"

"Why not indeed," I replied. "You have convinced me."

As she was heading for the wild food festival too, we agreed to visit it together. The festival site occupied a considerable acreage of grass, with tents and stalls offering an astonishing variety of foods. As well as the kind of wild food you might imagine: roasted wild pig, venison, fish from the lake, there were snails, fried cockroaches, crickets, and something called Prairie Oysters, a euphemism for bull's bollocks (testicles). Bush beer, and other exotic drinks made from berries and plants, and what looked like slimy bog water, was on sale for you to wash your bull's bollocks down if they stuck in your throat.

Wandering around, sampling some of this with my young Dutch friend, I received a slap on the back and a cheery greeting: "Watcher Mate!" I turned and there smiling at me was Carol Sutherland, a girl I had met in Scotland a couple of years before. She had helped crew for me on my yacht after I'd had a hernia operation. The doctor had wagged his finger at me and warned me, "There must be no single-handed sailing this summer! You must not sail unless you have a crew." And as luck would have it, a former colleague had come to crew for me for a long weekend and we had met Carol who had been serving in a fish and chips shop in Portree, Isle of Skye.

"What brings a girl from New Zealand to Skye to work in a fish and chip shop?" I asked.

"I'm backpacking around the world, working here for a spell to get some cash before I move on."

"Where are you going next?"

"Don't know. I'll wait and see what turns up?"

"How would you fancy a position as crew on a yacht cruising the west coast for the next three weeks? I have been forbidden to sail single-handed for medical reasons and this crew is leaving on Monday"

"Sounds great, when do we leave?"

That's how I acquired my crew and could go sailing - and two years later here she was slapping me on the back in a field in New Zealand. What an amazing coincidence that we should both be in the same small town on the other side of the world, on the same day, two years later.

"But how on earth did you find me in this crowd? I heard a radio report in the minibus that 20,000 people were expected to be here. And it looks like it too."

"Ah, but there is only one man here wearing a kilt, so you weren't difficult to find. I remembered from an email you sent that you would be touring around New Zealand at this time and I guessed this would be the kind of place to find you. I was visiting my father at Nelson and asked him to bring me down here. We are staying with an old friend who has a house in Hokitika. He has a spare room if you want to join us for dinner and an overnight stay."

Well, there you are: dinner, free accommodation, and a lift in her father's car up to Nelson the next day, with the offer of another night's hospitality there. I told you the New Zealanders were a friendly bunch. My young Dutch friend realised this was an offer I couldn't refuse. We shook hands and parted company. She was a remarkable girl.

And I was left wondering, if I had not been wearing my kilt, would Carol ever have found me in a crowd of 20,000 people?

Much of the following day was taken up with the drive north to Nelson. Carol's father knew someone with a yacht and arranged for me to have a sail with him the following afternoon, and while her father was preparing dinner, Carol drove me into town to give me a brief tour of the place she had been brought up in. A few miles along the road we passed an airfield with a sign: SKY-DIVING.

"Stop! Turn round and go in there. I want to go sky-diving." I said.

"Are you nuts?"

"Maybe, but if I don't do it now, I may regret it for the rest of my life. And it may be better to do it now, rather than wait and let me think about it."

But I had to wait. The last flight of the day had just landed and they were closing up for the night. "Be here at 9 o'clock tomorrow morning," the girl said.

That night I lay in bed thinking about it. Maybe I was nuts. What if the parachute didn't open, or the clip hitching my back to the chest of my tandem partner, an experienced sky-diver, broke? What if... they kept piling up. "Get a grip." I told myself. "Think of the probabilities," as I had done in the ocean when we thought we'd been abandoned to the sharks. The mathematician kicked in again and I reckoned the chances of something going wrong were a lot less risky than driving a car.

My tandem partner and I were the last of the three pairs to crawl into the tiny aircraft, and we would be the first to drop out. I was sitting on the floor, beside the door. Door? It was only a sheet of canvas! I couldn't even see out. When we reached the drop area, the canvas door was rolled up, and six inches from my backside was 12,000 feet of air space with a big chunk of New Zealand below it.

"Pivot around on your bum and let your legs dangle over the side," ordered my partner. "Now reach up, hold on to each side of the door, and wiggle your bum forward till you are right on the edge of the doorway."

When I had done that, he said, "Now let go and place your arms across your chest." He then eased himself forward and my entire body left the plane, still attached to him, hanging from a clip on his chest. It's interesting the thoughts that enter your head at a time like that. My future existence was in his power. "For heaven's sake don't fart now!" I thought. If I offended him, one flick of his finger could send me plunging to my death.

"Ready?"

"Yes."

The roar of the plane's engine died away and we were dropping like a stone, reaching a terminal velocity of around 120 miles per hour. I had enjoyed doing the calculations the night before - mathematics puts it all in perspective and soothes the troubled mind. To my surprise, I felt no feeling that I had left my stomach up there at 12, 000 feet while I dropped. The only sensation was the noise of the wind racing past my ears. And there below me was New Zealand, spread out like a map, and again contrary to my expectations, it did not shoot up towards me. Apart from the wind noise, it appeared as if we were hovering, motionless, enjoying the view, spreading our arms like a bird's wings, turning this way and that, and spinning around.

From nowhere, a girl with a video camera appeared in front of us. One of the staff, she had the most amazing ability to catch up with us, and divert to the other two couples, to film us as we dropped. And doing all this in free-fall. Using only her body to control her speed and direction of descent, she could manoeuvre from one group to the other, throughout the 9000 feet before we opened the parachutes. She was brilliant.

"Brace yourself for parachute," shouted my partner into my ear. A sudden jerk yanked us from a horizontal to a vertical position and the wind noise died at once. It seemed as if we had stopped, swinging in silence under the canopy above us. It was heavenly. I had mentioned that I needed to be at the harbour at 11a.m. to go sailing, so my partner fiddled with the parachute controls and took me out over the harbour, showing me the channel to the open sea, then we swung back over the town towards the airfield where the others were already landing. It was only as we made our final turn, about 100 feet up, that I had any sensation of the ground rising up to meet us. My man played the controls so that we made an approach like an aircraft landing, and as we skimmed low over the ground he said, "Bend your knees." Somehow, he put the brakes on and we came to a halt.

"Stand up and walk off." He clicked the bracket holding me to his chest and I walked free. Simple. As he gathered the parachute, I walked to the terminal building, my chest swelling with pride.

"How was it? " Asked the receptionist when she checked me in.

"Fantastic. The best thing since sex, but it's been so long since I had that, and I'm not sure if I can remember what it was like."

Once again, I thought of my young Dutch friend who had almost goaded me into doing it with her words: "Why not?"

Why not indeed! These two words have stayed with me and delivered many of life's most enjoyable experiences. Of course, you may feel some trepidation, fear even, but that can be overcome - and you don't need to be a mathematician to do a rough estimate of the probabilities to help you put things in perspective.

Feel the fear, but do it anyway.

Carol had intended to drive me to her home at Coromandel to show me around the North Island, but on the way to the ferry she received a phone call telling her to be in Perth, Western Australia, the following day to join a deep sea trawler about to head out to the

Southern Ocean fishing grounds. She worked as a fisheries observer for the government, checking and counting the catch of fish to ensure quotas and sustainable fishing practices were being observed.

"I'll give you the keys of my car and you can tour around in it and leave it at my house in Coromandel when you've finished," she said. I left her to pick up her flight tickets at Wellington and took the road north to the semi-tropical part of New Zealand.

This road trip was more of a touristic experience, sailing in the Bay of Islands and visiting the steaming geysers and hot mud springs at Rotorua.

Geyser, Rotorua

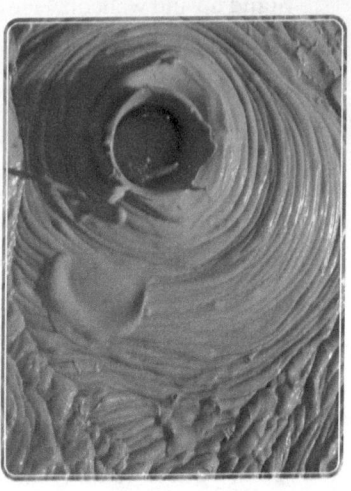

Hot mud spring, Rotorua

The highlight was a visit to Waipu where the House of Memories commemorates the settlement of a Scottish community there in the mid 19th century. The settlers had been led by a highland-born preacher, Norman MacLeod. A fundamentalist Presbyterian preacher, he had an extraordinary influence on his followers, taking over 160 of them - whole families - from the highlands of

Scotland to Pictou, Nova Scotia, and later to St Anns on Cape Breton Island. That is remarkable enough, but after 31 years there, finding the lifestyle becoming too worldly, he inspired his congregation to follow him to Australia. But to get to Australia they needed ships, several of them, to carry an entire community which now numbered around 800. But that was no problem. Among them were several boat builders, so they felled enough trees and set about building the ships they needed, then sailed the 12,000 miles to Adelaide.

After a short spell there, gold was discovered at Ballarat in the neighbouring state of Victoria and this led to a gold-rush. The lust for wealth and the greed it generated was condemned by the staunch Presbyterian minister, and Macleod then led his followers on yet another voyage to Waipu on the north east coast of New Zealand.

And there they settled, establishing a Gaelic-speaking Presbyterian community, maintaining their Scottish traditions. To this day, they remember their Scottish roots by holding a Highland Gathering, with the traditional hammer throwing, caber tossing, bagpiping, and highland dancing competitions.

The story of this remarkable man and his followers is told in a book: Norman MacLeod - Watchman Against the World, which I inherited after my father died. It is a memorable account of the passion of their beliefs, a remarkable leader, and the resourcefulness of a small highland community. And here I was, years after I had read their remarkable story, standing on the very spot where they had settled. The more you travel, the more you discover that the world is a large village.

And modern communications technology is making it feel even more so. In my previous book, Recapturing Youth, I described re-unions with three of my former pupils while traveling in Australia. One of these, Andrew Taylor, had contacted one of his classmates, Derek Todd, who was then living in Auckland. On hearing I had been tramping my way around the world, Derek, who had been a close friend of my son and was often in our house, had insisted that I come to visit him next time I was in Auckland. It was a delight to meet him again for a brief stay with his wife and family before I left to island-hop my way across the South Pacific.

CHAPTER 5

Prodigal Son

Fiji has over three hundred islands, and on this, my second visit, I fulfilled a desire to sail among some of them on the schooner, Seaspray, a classic yacht that achieved fame in a TV series, made in Australia in the late 1960s, about the adventures of a widowed journalist who travelled the Pacific with his three children. My voyage was executed in dream-like conditions under a cloudless sky. Ghosting along at a leisurely pace in the light wind, Seaspray combined the elegance of a bygone age with the graceful lines of a true thoroughbred.

The schooner, Seapray

First stop was at a rocky island where part of the film Castaway, starring Ton Hanks, was made. Ashore, the sand was so hot on the feet you couldn't stand on one spot and the heat stored in the black, volcanic rock was unbearable to walk on.

At nearby Malolo, a visit to an island village started with a welcoming kava-drinking ceremony with the local chief. The custom on such occasions is always to seek the chief's permission to enter the village. Visitors are expected to offer a gift, usually some kava root, but on this occasion we were invited to consider offering a cash donation to improve the resources of the local school.

After the formal welcome, we were free to roam the village and buy trinkets from the villagers: shells, hand-made jewellery, hats, woven mats, and tapa hangings (a sort of parchment made from bark) with traditional patterns dyed on them.

Housing was basic. The traditional style of house, the bure, is now being replaced by houses of concrete block construction with a tin roof. Windows eschewed the need for glazing: holes in the walls, with wooden shutters to provide some shade or protection in stormy conditions, were more than adequate in the hot climate. Doors were left open to encourage air circulation, and the houses had little in the way of furniture - often no more than mattresses laid on the concrete floor. Concrete, rather than wood, was preferred for the floors as it was cooler. Cooking was generally done outside over a wood fire, close to a rack with pots and a sink, or sometimes only a basin. Plumbing was elementary - a standpipe with a tap.

Traditional dwelling house

My main reason for coming back to Fiji was to return to Caqalai, the idyllic wee island I had lived on the previous year, to re-visit Kanai and his family who had looked after me so well after I had broken my Achilles Tendon. I was disappointed. The family had left the island a month before. Kanai, Dubai and the younger children were now living on the far side of Motoriki, a larger island nearby. No one knew where the girls, Dauni, Sherry, and Fanga, or Mopsje and the older boys were working now. The old chief had died, and the young chief and his wife were now running the island as a simple holiday resort, as it had been before.

I'm a sucker for the simple life on a wee island and stayed for five days. Because of my injury the previous year, I hadn't been very active. This time I made up for it, exploring the island - that only took about half an hour - exploring Leluvia, a neighbouring island, and snorkelling. The snorkelling was outstanding with some of the most vibrant coral gardens I have ever seen.

As had happened the previous year when we went over to Motoriki for the Sunday church service, the chief asked me to speak on behalf of the visitors. Most of the congregation not only recognised me, they even remembered my name, and when the service was over I received a heart-warming welcome. The minister's wife hugged me and beamed at me.

"John, this is wonderful. You have travelled all the way round the world, yet you have come back to us again. That means a lot to us."

To my astonishment, the chief ordered a special kava-drinking ceremony to celebrate my return. We all retired to the village hall and I was given the place of honour, seated cross-legged on the floor, in my kilt, immediately opposite the chief. The local people and visitors arranged themselves in a circle around us. As always, the chief was offered the first cup of kava, in his own personal half-coconut shell. As guest of honour, I was offered the next half-coconut shell filled with the muddy-looking liquid. The cup then circulated among the others. It had proved to be quite a homecoming. I felt like the Prodigal Son.

With a few days left before I was due to leave Fiji, I decided to have a look at the Yasawa islands on the western frontier of Fiji. A tourist brochure at the ferry booking agent's office had a page labelled Coconut Bay, describing 'a small resort owned by Sherry and her family.' I remembered Sherry telling me the previous year on Caqalai that her family owned a small resort on one of the Yasawa Islands. If Sherry were there now I could perhaps get news of the others from her. I asked the tour agent to phone Coconut Bay and ask if Sherry was on the island. No luck. The Coconut Bay phone was out of order.

However, the agent called a neighbouring resort. They confirmed Sherry was on the island and they were willing to pass on a message telling her that a guest called John was coming for three nights. I did not offer any further details. I wanted it to be a surprise, and reserved a place on the ferry to the island for the next morning. As events unfolded, there were more surprises for *me*.

With no harbour on the island, passengers are transferred to small boats and taken to the shore, where they have to wade through the shallows to the beach. When a small motorboat came alongside the ferry at Coconut Bay, I gasped when I saw the helmsman. It was Mopsje, who had ferried me to and from Caqalai the previous year. Once he had the boat lashed alongside, he looked up and reached out to catch my baggage. I stuck my hand out instead and shook his, grinning.

"Hi Mopsje!"

"John!" he gasped. He was speechless. So was I, in my delight to see him again. The usual welcoming party awaited my arrival on the shore: three boys playing guitars and singing, with Sherry beside them, looking out towards us. When she recognised the newcomer, she screamed, ran back up the beach, and rushed into the kitchen. When she came back out, she was dragging Dauni behind her and they both rushed down the beach. I jumped out of the boat and waded ashore into their open arms.

"How did you know we were here?" asked Dauni.

"I didn't." I then explained the sequence of events; my going to Caqalai, the disappointment to learn they had all left, and finding the leaflet that led me here. They were astounded that I had found them again.

"Oh, John," asserted Dauni, "you can't ignore this. It's the hand of God guiding you back here to marry me!"

I laughed. "Well, maybe He did guide me here, but I'm not so sure about the marriage bit."

Sherry and Mopsje had become husband and wife and were now expecting a child. That afternoon, as I lay reading on a hammock slung between two trees, a girl walked past. She stopped dead in her tracks, staring at me. "Excuse me, sir. Is your name John?"

"Aye." It was Niko, one of the kitchen maids from Caqalai. She told me that Anna, another of the kitchen girls, was also here. Having been reunited with five of the young people who cared for me so well the previous year, I just had to stay for longer than the two nights I had planned.

To change my flights and get more cash to cover the cost of my extended stay necessitated a trip back to the mainland. Mopsje and Sherry were going over to the hospital for a routine check on her pregnancy in a couple of days and Dauni was going too for some food supplies, so I went with them. Forty miles in the small open boat - in a thunderstorm! The two girls and I lay on an improvised mattress of lifejackets on the floor of the boat and covered ourselves with a tarpaulin while Mopsje stayed at the tiller and got soaked. I wondered what it would feel like if lightning struck us, but the fact that you are reading this proves we made it without being incinerated.

We stayed overnight at Dauni's sister's house in Lautoka. She and her husband and children had come to Caqalai at Christmas the previous year when I had played my spoons on the childrens' knees. That had ensured my immortality, and recognition was instant: "Did you bring your spoons?"

This reunion called for another celebration - more kava drinking! I feigned great enthusiasm and joined in the fun. They were so hospitable and insisted that when I had to leave Fiji I was to come to their house again for a feast and kava, to stay overnight, and they would drive me to the airport for my morning flight.

Next day I re-scheduled my tickets, and we shipped the supplies back to Coconut Bay. I could now relax and enjoy myself among friends.

CHAPTER 6

Faith & Hope

During my extended stay, I became familiar with the island and was pressurised into entertaining the other visitors. Spending a lot of time in the sea, diving and snorkelling on the local reef, I had found underwater caves that even the local boys didn't know existed. They went out to spear-fish for food, whereas I spent time exploring the reef. I was therefore asked to guide groups who wanted to go snorkelling. That gave the boys more time to fish.

The underwater caves were beautiful. Encrusted with marine growths, the cave walls were a muted pink with shellfish and soft corals clinging to them. Sunlight beamed down through holes in the coral and was reflected from the sandy bottom, creating an ethereal, bluish glow that illuminated the caves.

Guiding a group of snorkelers, I indicated to them to watch while I dived to the bottom, about six metres down, and disappeared into a cave I knew well. Emerging through an exit hole in the reef some distance behind the snorkelers, I waited while they watched the mouth of the cave, expecting to see me reappear from there. When I didn't, they became agitated. I swam over and tapped one on the head.

"Where did you come from? We thought you had become trapped in there and drowned," he cried.

By then, I had become a temporary unpaid member of the resort staff, leading groups through the bush and over the hill to the next bay for picnics, dining on freshly-speared fish cooked on a wood fire. Another job was demonstrating how to gather and husk coconuts. It started when the Fijian boys asked me to do their usual talk about the coconut palm and its usefulness to the islanders.

"You already know all the facts and your English is much better than ours," they reasoned. When they saw I could climb a coconut tree as well, they thought it would be a good idea for the visitors to see that even a white man could survive here. Having climbed the tree and brought down the nuts, I then completed the demonstration by husking the nuts and cracking them open, while the local boys, who should have been doing this work, lay back and relaxed. I didn't mind a bit. I was a boy again, enjoying my recaptured youth.

Coconut tree demonstration

A group of us took a trip to the other side of the island to visit the secondary school. The teacher of a class of 15 and 16 year-olds asked us to introduce ourselves, tell the students where we came from, and what we did for a living. The students sat and listened. The Fijians are enthusiastic about rugby, and several of the group mentioned rugby as one of their interests. In my youth I had played football. Proper football. The beautiful game. Where the magic is performed with the feet. And to demonstrate, I began to mime the art of ball juggling with feet, knees, head, and shoulders. Big, white-toothed grins broke out. The kids were fascinated by every flick and nod. They gazed at the artistry with which I kept this non-existent ball in the air. For the climax, I flicked the ball up from foot to head, nodded it a couple of times, then bounced it off my left shoulder on to my right knee, which gave it another flick upwards. As it dropped towards the floor, I swung my right leg behind my left leg and volleyed the ball into the middle of the class - except that there *was* no ball! It was all imaginary.

Yet so engrossed were they, when I propelled the non-existent ball into the crowd, one boy was so tuned-in he reached up and caught it, like a goalkeeper, bringing a spontaneous round of applause from the rest of the class. Even the other tourists clapped. Such is the power of imagination. It's one of the first principles of teaching: stimulate the imagination and you capture their attention. Then the learning can begin.

Before we left, the students sang for us, unaccompanied. They had no need for musical instruments. One girl hit the first note and the rest followed, singing beautiful harmonies. In common with the other people in the Pacific islands, music is in their soul.

We waved goodbye and filed out. "Goodbye!" they called and waved. Then one girl called out, "Goodbye, *John!*" Another followed suit, and then came a chorus of "Goodbye, *John!*"

My ball juggling had made quite an impression - it would never have been so good if I'd actually had a ball! What mattered was that they believed in something they could not see. That's faith.

Now, take me to the sea and I'll show you how to walk on water!

Yet again, I found myself cast into the unexpected role of counsellor to damsels in distress. The Fijian boys had a good thing going there. Every day, new girls came to the island to stay for a few days, so there was an endless stream of young ladies for the boys to charm. Their well-toned muscles, abilities as hunter-gatherers, their skills at volleyball, at which they always out-performed the visitors, never failed to impress. Each night they played guitars, sang love songs, and demonstrated traditional dances.

To this heady cocktail of skill, virility, and ethnic charm, add the moonlight shimmering over the bay and the whispering of a soft breeze among the palms, and it's hardly surprising that some of the young ladies succumbed to the amorous advances of these young Fijian bucks. Perhaps that's why these boys were too tired to climb coconut trees!

Coconut Bay sunset

After a quick fling for a couple of days, the girls left to continue their travels. But when liaisons with the local guys became a wee bit complicated and the girls needed someone to listen to their romantic problems, they came to me for advice. And it wasn't only the girls. Late one afternoon, I was approached by one of the young Fijian stallions, the Alpha Male of the village, no less. A smooth operator, he had just returned from an afternoon walk along the beach with one of the tourist girls. He looked around furtively and muttered, "Can I have a quick word with you, John? Could you lend me a condom?" Here was exactly the same thing happening to me again as had happened the previous year on Caqalai!

"Aye, sure," I replied, and fished one out from the same stock, still unused, by *me*.

"Thanks John, I was sure I could count on you." And he shot off with a big grin on his face. But why did he come to me? What made him think I would have one? He too had faith in me!

A couple of hours later I went for dinner. He came in to do duty as a waiter, smiled at me, winked, and flashed the 'okay' hand signal used by divers. His hopes had been realised. His faith in me had been justified.

On my last night on the island as I sat on the beach watching the sun setting over the bay, Chiko, a vivacious Japanese girl, came and sat beside me. A few days earlier she had sought my advice on dealing with a local boy she had become involved with. He wanted her to stay and marry him, but she was only having some holiday fun. I let her talk to ease her mind, asked a few questions, and let her decide for herself how to handle the situation. She had regained control, dampened the ardour of her suitor, and we had become good friends. Together we sat and watched the sun slip below the horizon.

"That's a sight I'm going to miss when I leave." I said.

"And I'm going to miss *you*, John. I don't know what I'll do without you." She reached out, touched my arm, and stroked it gently. "You're a really cool guy, John."

"Oh?" With this 'really cool guy' stuff, and stroking my arm, I wondered where was this heading.

"I would like to keep in touch with you, John."

"Aye, no problem. I'll give you my email address."

"That's cool, but I would like more than that. Have you ever thought of visiting Japan? Would you would like to come and visit me in Okinawa?"

"Aye, why not?"

"Oh John, that would be so cool!" She squeezed my arm with delight, her eyes sparkling in the dying light of the sun. "You could stay with me. I could show you around and be your interpreter."

Well, this is getting better all the time, I'm thinking. This girl has obviously had enough of these rampant young Fijian bucks. She has discovered that the more mature man has something better to offer: wisdom and understanding, stimulating conversation, tenderness, and some vintage-quality experience. Maybe, as it's my last night here, she's keen to make the most of the time left; otherwise she might be left wondering what if…? This was beyond my wildest hopes.

I reached out and touched her arm. Her skin was smooth as silk. I stroked it, mirroring her touch on mine. "I would love to come and spend time with you in Okinawa, Chiko."

Her eyes glistened with emotion. She gasped, "Oh John, that would be wonderful! Because I want you… to be the *grandfather* I never knew!"

Grandfather? Everything drooped after that.

CHAPTER 7

Samoa

As the plane took off from Fiji, a kaleidoscope of colours unfolded below: the deep blue of the ocean's depths, the browns, reds and golden colours of coral reefs, lush, green islands fringed with white beaches and turquoise lagoons. I marvelled at the risks taken by the first European ships to navigate these uncharted waters, for scattered among Fiji's three hundred or more islands lie even more coral reefs - beautiful, but deadly to the unwary mariner.

Samoa (not to be confused with American Samoa, a different set of islands, not far off) consists of two large volcanic islands, Upolu and Savai'i, with a sprinkling of tiny islands close by. From the air, the volcanic nature of Savai'i becomes obvious with well-defined craters and extensive lava fields. The last eruption in 1911 lasted for six years. Upolu is more heavily forested. On both islands, most of the population live along a narrow coastal strip in a series of villages. Apia, the capital, is the only city in Samoa.

The main attraction in Apia for me was Villa Vailima, the former home of the 19th century Scottish novelist, Robert Louis Stevenson. The last four years of his life were spent in this imposing mansion house, built on an elevated site overlooking the city. The author of such classics as *Treasure Island, The Strange*

Tale of Doctor Jekyll and Mr Hyde, Kidnapped, The Bodysnatchers, he had been dogged by ill health and had spent two years cruising among the Pacific islands in a schooner with his wife and extended family of in-laws. He fell in love with Samoa, settled there, and built this fine house.

Villa Vailima

Known in Samoa as Tusitala (Storyteller), he won the respect and affection of the Samoans. Following a guided tour of Villa Vailima, I visited Stevenson's grave on top of a neighbouring hill. A steep hill covered in jungle, climbing it was energy sapping in such a hot climate. The fact that Samoan coffin bearers carried his body to his lofty grave demonstrates the depth of feeling they had for him. On the grave are the words he composed as his own epitaph:

> *Under the wild and starry sky*
> *Dig the grave and let me die*
> *Glad did I live and gladly die*

And I laid me down with a will
This be the verse you grave for me
Here he lies where he longed to be
Home is the sailor home from the sea
And the hunter home from the hill.

The most reliable way to get around the islands is to negotiate a personal tour through a local agency. You can be picked up by minibus each day and dropped off at your chosen destination, with accommodation and food all included in the price. This avoids potential problems with the public transport on Samoa. Buses run according to the whims of the driver, who may own the bus, and he sets his own timetable. If he meets a friend who is about to go out for a day's fishing and takes a notion to accompany him, then he'll leave the bus and his passengers to fend for themselves. Passengers then have to wait for another bus, which will come whenever *its* driver decides. With limited time, I preferred not to experience that aspect of local culture.

My arrangements worked well. It was the same driver each day, one for each island. The drivers were informative, knew the hosts, and we became known to each other as the days progressed. Some houses are modern concrete block bungalows, but the traditional falle, (a house without walls, basically just a roof supported on posts), is still very much in evidence. The concept of privacy seems to have eluded the Samoans as the falle has neither exterior, nor interior, walls. You can look right through a house from the street, see the furniture sitting there, with TV, cookers, and fridges. I wonder to what extent this contributes to the nature of the Samoans: a people, open and honest, among whom crime is almost unknown and material possessions are accorded much less importance than in western society. In the poorer falles the only furnishings were a few mats and a mattress. The kitchen was sometimes an external shelter with earthen floor and an open wood fire. Families eat using their fingers, seated cross-legged on the floor.

Samoa, in terms of housing and customs, is more traditional than any of the other island groups I had visited. Religion exerts a powerful influence. A bell is rung in each village every evening at around 6:45 p.m. This is the signal that it is time for family prayers. Visitors walking through the village at that time are asked to respect this custom and sit by the roadside until the bell is rung again, after about twenty minutes, to signify that devotions have ended.

My first day took me around the east side of Upolu where I was picked up by a small boat and ferried out to Nu'utele, a tiny rocky island for my overnight stay. I was greeted at the beach by Fa'anati, a pleasant 21 year-old girl, who took me to my falle and prepared my bed and mosquito net for me, interrogating me as she did so with the inevitable: "Travelling alone? No wife? Do you have a girlfriend?"

I decided to play the same game. "Have you got a boyfriend? No? Surely there must be plenty of young Samoan men who would love to go out with you?"

"They're no good. Too lazy. My father doesn't want me to marry a local boy. He told me to get a foreign husband. They take better care of their wives than Samoan men." I recalled my friend Ray's similar words in Suva the previous year about Fijian women preferring European men. She then invited me for a cup of tea. Her cousin, a woman in her thirties, joined us and started asking the same questions.

My falle

"Why don't you marry a Samoan girl? Fa'anati would like a husband. She is a good cook and would take good care of you. She's very good at massage. Take her round the island and let her give you a massage."

Was massage a euphemism for something else? I began to break out in a sweat - and it wasn't the tea that raised my temperature - and changed the subject.

That evening, Fa'anati beat a tattoo on a large wooden drum to summon the guests to dinner. I wore my kilt and when I walked across to the dining area, a cheer erupted from the other guests and the two boys who worked on the island. In response, I started my Maori warrior dance. Fa'anati's eyes lit up, she passed the drum sticks to her brother and began to dance along with me, hips shaking to the rhythm of the drums. When the music stopped I planted a kiss on her cheek. She giggled, and went off to serve dinner.

After dinner, the staff went back to the mainland, leaving only the owner and his wife on the island with the guests. As I walked down to the beach with the boys to see them off, Fa'anati's brother sidled up to me and whispered, "We'll bring your girlfriend back later, John."

"Eh? What girlfriend?" The boy looked at me as if I was thick, which, it must be obvious by now, I am. Very.

"Your girlfriend," he hissed. "Fa'anati!"

"Oh. Is she my girlfriend?"

"Of course," he muttered. "She told us she likes you, so we'll bring her back later tonight so you can be together."

"Oh, that's very kind of you," I mumbled. They all climbed into the boat and pushed off. As the engine roared into life I waved. They all waved back.

"See you later, John," the boy called out and nodded to his sister. Fa'anati turned to look at him, then she looked back at me, and blew me a kiss. I blew one back. She beamed and waved to me.

The moon was rising over the horizon. The sky was perfectly clear. Silvery moonlight shimmered over the lagoon, palm leaves swayed overhead, and the swish of waves whispering along the beach created a perfect night for romance.

But the boat did not return, and I fell asleep with my fantasies. When I left in the morning, Fa'anati gave me a hug and slipped me a piece of paper with her address on it, and asked me to write. I began to wonder what might have happened if I'd stayed around a bit longer.

At my next stop, I slept in a falle built among the branches of a tree above the beach. The three teenagers, two boys and a girl in the family who owned it, were full of questions. They were keen to improve their English, and they helped me with the Samoan language. The guest's dinner was usually brought from the family house to the falle, but that night I was invited to join the family in their home for the evening meal, and to join them in their evening devotions. Every night they sit on the floor and conduct a short religious service: a Bible reading by one of the sons, a prayer led by another, and singing led by the daughter. Parents and grandparents were present, and all sang in an occasion marked by a simplicity and sincerity that far outshone the extravagant display of pomp and ceremony so often seen in formal religious ceremonies. The words of Robert Burns, Scotland's National Bard, came to mind:

> *Compared with this, how poor Religion's pride,*
> *In all the pomp of method, and of art;*
> *Where men display to congregations wide*
> *Devotion's every grace - except the heart!*

Before dinner was served, I was invited to offer a short prayer of thanksgiving before eating. A small bowl of water was brought to me to wash my hands, and the food was then served. Afterwards, the boys' guitars came out and I joined in with my spoons: the young ones had ordered me to bring them. The grandparents, both looking very infirm and lying on their beds, had to be helped to eat, but on hearing the clatter of the spoons they both forced themselves upright and beamed with delight. The grandmother's hands clapped in time to the music to the extent that her loose fitting nightdress slipped off her right shoulder revealing a long sagging breast, but she didn't give a hoot. She was enjoying herself.

I was packing my rucksack when my bus driver arrived to pick me up next morning. While he waited, my host chatted with him for a few minutes and told him of the evening before. As we drove off the driver told me, "John, you made a great impression there.

You are the first tourist ever to have been invited to join them for the evening meal in their house. That is a great honour."

At the next village, while I was taking some photographs, a woman called me over. I wondered if I had caused offence by taking pictures without permission, but no, she was charming and was curious about me. She asked all the usual questions, leading to the inevitable, "Why not marry a nice Samoan girl?"

With the help of her niece, she was preparing food in her cooking falle, a simple earth-floored kitchen with a log fire and a wooden fence round it to keep the pigs out. Having satisfied her curiosity about me, she was also responsive to my questions about her lifestyle and culture. My preference for doing something, rather than just sitting around, amused her, so she let me help in the preparation of the food. Her husband showed me how to grate the coconut and press the gratings in a wrap of tough grass to make coconut cream. It was added to a large stewpot on the fire with the hunks of pork the woman and her niece had been chopping. Vegetables were added and the mix left to stew for a while. They were delighted with my interest in their way of life, were equally curious about mine, and took great pleasure in having their photographs taken.

Of course, having learned that I was available, the woman suggested I should marry her 22 year-old niece, Tina, who didn't seem at all put out by the idea. But I had to move on next morning. I began to regret the fact that I was on a tour. How much more interesting might it be if I were to stay put in one village, become absorbed in the community, and allow interactions to take place. Like Robert Louis Stevenson, I might never have left.

To my surprise, they too invited me to join them for dinner. I felt a bit hesitant as this was an impoverished family. Only a month before, their falle had been destroyed by a cyclone and had not yet been rebuilt. They were sleeping in the husband's parents' falle. But they would not take no for an answer, and again I was treated as an honoured guest. The woman would not eat until I had finished. Her duty was to remain in attendance, serving me food till I had eaten my fill, waving a leaf about to keep the flies off me. These humble people impressed me: in material terms they had little, yet spiritually they were rich.

Snorkelling had been disappointing in Samoa. Most of the shallow water coral was dead, having suffered from the recent cyclone; but I felt sure that wasn't the only reason. I wondered if the crown of thorns starfish had been responsible for the devastation I witnessed, but I never saw one, perhaps because they had cleaned the place out already. I arranged a couple of dives with a local operator who took me to a very good site off the south coast. We dived down thirty metres to the bottom of a tall coral pinnacle and spiralled our way round it, ascending back to the surface. This was a rich habitat with healthy coral and abundant fish life. Two large sharks spotted us and diverted seawards. We swam round behind the pinnacle and encountered them once more. Crouching behind some coral, we watched. Scouting around, their movements were effortless and graceful, their bodies sleek and streamlined. As soon as we revealed ourselves they gave a flip of the tail and disappeared into the gloom. A turtle finned its way across in front of us, quite unconcerned about our presence; a school of sleek tuna darted past. It was wonderful to be underwater again.

After dinner, I walked along the beach to a neighbouring resort to see a demonstration of fire-dancing on the beach. The dining room of the resort was open-sided, with the audience facing outwards to the beach. As I approached, the drums began, the signal that the show was about to commence, and a woman in traditional costume appeared on the sand, said a few words of welcome, and retreated into the shadows. The audience, seated in the bright light of the dining room, looked out to the sand. But instead of a group of fire dancers, a Scotsman wearing a kilt emerged from the gloom. I strode into the light, and into the dining room. People gasped and turned to gaze in wonder.

The manager approached me, grasped my hand, and introduced himself. He was from New York.

"That was one of the most remarkable entrances I have ever seen!" he cried. "The woman faded into the shadows and, like Brigadoon, you emerged out of the mists in full highland dress. It was stunning! Where did you come from?" He then insisted that I take a seat in the dining room to watch the show.

As usual, at the end of the performance they invited a few of the visitors to dance with them - and after an entrance like that it was inevitable that I would be one of them. I had never seen Samoan dancing before, but I improvised, injecting a bit of Cook Island style dancing. That went down well. When we had finished, my dancing partner shook my hand, kissed my cheek, and murmured, "Hey, you're cool!"

The manager was waiting at my table with a glass of beer in his hand. "John, please accept this with the compliments of the house for your outstanding performance. Your presence has enhanced the entertainment tonight."

"That's very kind of you. Cheers!" I needed that beer. Dancing in the tropics is hot work, especially when wearing a kilt.

A short trip by ferry took me to Savai'i. A larger island than Upolo, its high volcanic interior is uninhabited. My new minibus driver met me at the jetty and took me to the resort. My falle was still being prepared for me, but I had the company of two charming young ladies at reception who entertained me with conversation.

Leaning against the counter with one arm resting on its surface while chatting to the girl on my side of the desk, I became aware of a hand stroking my forearm. I turned and there was the girl on the other side of the desk engrossed in stroking the hairs on my arm. I paused in my conversation and that broke the spell. She withdrew her hand and apologised.

"Och, there's no need to apologise. I was enjoying it," I protested. I reached out, took her hand and placed it back on my arm. "Now you keep caressing me for as long as you like."

She laughed. "Oh, it's just so strange to see such a hairy arm. Men here don't have hairs on their arms like that. It's lovely and soft to touch."

"Well, be my guest. Stroke away," I commanded, but the housemaid came to tell me my falle was ready and the sensual welcome was over.

I was the only guest in the resort that night. The owner, a Samoan woman who had lived in New Zealand for many years, invited me to join her and her husband for dinner. They were good company, and when they left to catch up on some office work, they instructed their young staff to keep me entertained. The girl from reception who'd stroked my arm came over and joined me, much to my delight.

A long drive over the extensive lava fields took us to a village built around the edge of an extinct low-level crater about 200 metres in diameter. Here was an example of nature's creation turned to good advantage. The floor of the crater was flat, so the Samoans had converted it into a rugby stadium. The inner slopes of the crater provided terracing for spectators and almost every house in the village looked over the crater, offering a view of the games. Brilliant.

My plan had been to dive a couple of sites around the coast of Savai'i, but this coast had been devastated by a recent cyclone. High seas had breached coastal roads, houses had been destroyed, boats damaged. Palm trees had been stripped of their foliage and stood forlorn, bare as match sticks, every frond and coconut having been carried off by the wind. Recovery work was in progress all along the coast, but no dive boats were yet operating so my plans were scuppered. The next few days were spent in uncharacteristic idleness.

All across the Pacific the people are very musical. During dinner at one resort, three musicians played guitars, with another playing a single-string base made from a plastic bucket and a broom handle. These guys were good. I asked if I could join in with spoons. No problem. The audience clapped like mad and wouldn't let me rest after that. I also belted out some blues on harmonica and another Samoan in the audience, now living in the USA, joined in on guitar. He was another ace player and his wife was an excellent singer.

One of life's great pleasures is when a few musicians come together, unrehearsed, and provide entertainment that delights an audience. Our jam session went on till 1:30 a.m. and before leaving, I apologised for keeping the waitresses up late. They had kept me supplied with free beer all night, my reward for providing entertainment. "Oh, there's no need to apologise. We're looking forward to more of the same tomorrow night."

"I won't be here tomorrow night. I have to move on."

"Oh no! Can't you stay for just one more night?"

"I wish I could, but my arrangements are made. I would love to stay, but I am expected at another resort tomorrow."

"Oh, you'll have to come back. That was the best night we've had here for years."

Again I regretted my decision to keep moving on, but there was no way of knowing what I would find in each village. On my last day on Savai'i I had plenty of time before catching a late afternoon flight back to Upolo. My driver had no other customers to pick up and offered to show me some interesting places along the way.

He led me to a waterfall where we took a refreshing swim in the pool below the falls, after which we went to a spot on the coast where the lava flow ended in the sea. This part is notable for its blowholes. The waves are funnelled up inside lava tubes, and being compressed as the tubes narrow, when they strike the end of the tube the spray is ejected from holes in the rock some distance back from the water's edge with sufficient power to propel a coconut dropped into it about thirty metres (100 feet) up into the air.

I recalled reading R M Ballantyne's classic story, *The Coral Island*, when I was about ten years old. The first story I had read of life in the South Pacific, it had left powerful images in my mind. One part described such blowholes and I began to wonder where Ballantyne got his inspiration. Had he been here too, standing at this exact spot in the middle of the nineteenth century? I did some checking on the internet and discovered that he had indeed been to Samoa. I had already visited many of the places associated with Captain Cook, traced much of Robert Louis Stevenson's route, and now I found myself following in the footsteps of another Scottish writer whose descriptions had sparked my longing to see the South Pacific islands so many years before.

Samoa swimming pool

These stories had created images in my young mind. These images had become my personal property, and were possibly different from those in the minds of other readers of the same stories. Had I only seen film or a TV dramatisation would the images have remained so powerful? I have my doubts, for then they would have been the creation of someone else's imagination. Such is the power of literature.

I enjoyed my visit to Samoa, but my journey round the islands had reinforced the message that a rolling stone gathers no moss. I'd had to make a decision between staying in one place and wondering what was around the corner, or having a quick dash round the islands, seeing much, but perhaps gaining little. My experiences in Fiji and on Rarotonga had taught me that considerable enrichment could be gained from lingering awhile in one place, savouring the lifestyle and culture of its people. I would have loved to have spent more time in Samoa, but even though my stays in each village were short, I had gained much from the humble and hospitable people I had met.

CHAPTER 8

Savaged

Arriving at Rarotonga airport, you step off the plane on to the tarmac, and walking across to the terminal you inhale the fragrant tropical breeze which caresses this island and titillates the senses. Brown-faced, stocky men driving luggage trolleys are waiting for the cargo hold doors to open. They look over, curious to see who has arrived, smile, nod, and call out their greeting, "Kia Orana" – May you live on. Having cleared immigration and collected my baggage from the carousel, I entered the arrivals hall.

"John! John!" I looked to my left and there was Krystina, the teenage girl who had earned the title, Miss Tiare, at the annual flower festival the previous year, running over to hug me. She was waiting for her brother who was on the same flight and was surprised to see me walk off it. Her mother and father came over to greet me, and behind them was Mata from Tiare Village waiting to pick me up in the minibus, all smiles and fragrance, wearing her head ei, a beautifully crafted crown of bright, sweet-smelling flowers. Three more beaming Cook Island ladies followed in quick succession with hugs and smiles, all delighted that I had returned. It felt good to be back.

After checking in at the hostel, I went to a wee shop along the road for some provisions for breakfast. I almost collided with a young woman at the door. Her eyes opened wide. "John! When did you get back?" Another big hug. Fiona was the daughter of Rob Good, a Scotsman who had married a Cook Islander. "Oh, Dad and Mum will be delighted to see you again. You must go and surprise them."

I did, the following night. Their house was only a few minutes walk away, so I put on my kilt and walked along the darkened road. Only one car passed me. It stopped. The reversing lights came on and it reversed towards me. Bet it's a woman, I thought. Not just one woman; she had four young ladies with her.

"Excuse me sir, would you like a lift?"

"Thanks. That's very kind of you, but I'm only going another twenty yards to visit a fellow Scotsman."

"Which one?"

"Rob Good."

"Oh, you know Uncle Rob and Aunt Mary then."

It seems everybody I meet on Rarotonga is related to someone I know. As she explained her Scottish ancestry, I gazed at the four girls inside, all smiling at me. What a fool! I could have squeezed in there beside them instead of going to see old Rob. However, Mary is an excellent baker and always stuffs me with goodies when I call - and she gave me some to take away with me.

Christine, a Malaysian final-year medical student, occupied the other bedroom in the chalet. A bundle of energy and enthusiasm, from the moment we met we got on very well. She was also a diver, so we formed a buddy team to explore the reefs around Rarotonga, and on her first few nights out she had been comfortable to have me as chaperone and guide. With just the two of us in the chalet, we shared in the cooking, alternating duties night about, so we could learn culinary arts from each other. She was good company and I have to confess, for the first time in my life, I slept with a girl on the first day we met.

Now hold on!

Don't get carried away with images of torrid nights of passion under the palms. My use of language is precise. The truth is, when we got back to Tiare Village after attending the Island Night show of traditional music and dance on her first night, we couldn't open the door of the chalet. Christine had flicked the security catch on when she closed the door on the way out, so it could only be opened from the inside - and there was no one inside to open it.

It was now almost 1 a.m. Adrienne didn't live on-site and would not have been pleased to be wakened at that time of night. A not too comfy settee in the hostel lounge could sleep one of us, but the other would have to lie on the floor. Christine was noble enough to suggest tossing a coin to decide who gets the settee. However, a better plan formed in my mind.

Another couple had come back with us. They were the only occupants of the neighbouring chalet in which there was an unoccupied room. In these A-Frame chalets the rooms upstairs were only partitioned. With the aid of a chair, you could haul yourself up and over the partition, drop down, and open the door from the inside. The other couple allowed us into their chalet. I scrambled over the partition into the twin bedroom and Christine and I spent the night there - but in separate beds! Christine behaved with the utmost propriety and never interfered with me at all.

I enjoyed telling Adrienne in the morning that I had broken into a bedroom and slept with one of her guests. She laughed, much to my relief, and with the aid of a power drill she unscrewed the security guard from the window of Christine's bedroom, removed the slatted panes of glass, and Christine climbed in and opened the door from the inside.

Next day, I was gazing at a menu board outside a café, contemplating a snack for lunch when once more I heard a startled cry. "John! You've come back!" I looked up and Amina, a pretty young waitress, came forward and hugged me. And people keep asking me why I return to this island!

As usual on Thursdays, I had organised a party from the hostel to attend the Island Night Show at the Staircase Restaurant. After the Polynesian feast, we sat back to watch the dance show. Danny Mataroa, the Master of Ceremonies, welcomed everyone as usual, but then added, "And a special welcome to our friend John, from Scotland, who is back with us again."

After the show finished, a young islander in his mid-twenties came over to our table. "John! It's great to see you back. You must come out on the deck and meet the rest of the boys. They'll be delighted to see you again." I followed him out to the open-air deck extending outwards from the dining room and three other young men looked up. Their faces broke into big grins and they reached out to slap my hand and hug me.

Tere, my old friend, was almost turning somersaults: erupting with laughter, bringing his knee up and slapping it. He then grasped my hand, shaking it, hugging me, slapping my back.

He paused and looked at me again. "I can't believe it. You're here again. What a guy!" And then the whole hand-slapping, hand-shaking, back-slapping, and hugging was repeated. After a few minutes, the girls from the hostel who'd accompanied me became curious and joined us. That made the local lads happier still. Introductions complete, the guys and gals got boogieing and the party began to swing.

I had planned a three-month stay to do some voluntary work, so I decided to buy a second-hand motorbike rather than hire one. I could sell it again when I left the island. I went to the bank to withdraw cash to pay for it.

As I handed over my card for a cash advance, the girl behind the desk looked at me and smiled. "So, you've come back again, John." I was taken aback.

"Aye....," I muttered. She was quick to notice.

"You don't remember me, do you?" The words were terse, fired at me like a burst from a machine gun. Ouch.

"Well... your face is familiar. I'm trying to remember where I've seen you before, but it wasn't in here." I had always used the cash machine before.

"That's right. But you don't even remember my name? Oh well, I couldn't have made much of an impression then." She feigned offence. At least, I think she was pretending. Pretending or not, she had me squirming.

"Och, wait a minute. Look, I meet so many beautiful young ladies here and it's difficult to remember all their names." Well, that did no good at all.

"Oh, so you remember some of them, but not me! So all that talk about being your favourite waitress meant nothing at all." This lassie had the knife in the wound, and she was twisting it. I writhed in agony and struggled with my memories....Waitress?

"Wait a minute! I've got you now. You were a waitress at the Edgewater Hotel." It was a place I sometimes frequented for dinner and to see traditional dance shows. She had been working there some evenings for extra income.

"Oh, so you do remember me.... at last." This lassie could make a man suffer. And just to set the record straight, all that stuff about the 'favourite waitress' - I'm sure I had never used a corny chat-up line like in all my life. She was just being creative, and I admired her for it.

"You're making me feel terrible," I spluttered.

"And so you should be. I was so pleased to see you, expected that you'd be pleased to see me too, but you didn't even recognise me. Well…"

"Och, look, I'm really sorry. What can I do to make amends?"

Quick as a flash, she rapped out, "Well, I suppose you could buy me lunch."

"I'd be delighted to…" But before I could finish, she fired back.

"But I don't think I want to have lunch with a man who doesn't even recognise me. There's your money now. You can go and do your shopping and forget all about me again."

I loved this girl's sense of humour, her quick wit, and her play-acting - at least I think she was play-acting! It was game, set, and match to her. I took my cash and left with my tail between my legs.

But my conscience was bothering me. She was rather sweet in an acerbic sort of way, and pretty. Should I go back in again and insist on taking her for lunch? But it might be like walking into a lion's den. I would hate to be savaged twice.

CHAPTER 9

Celebrity

Although English is spoken throughout the Cook Islands, some children struggle with reading and writing the language, and many homes are without books. The education department could not afford to pay for learning support specialists so I offered myself for a full term, unpaid. As the head of a school I'd had experience in setting up support schemes for pupils with learning difficulties. My offer was accepted.

I enjoyed being back working at grass-roots level, much of the time tutoring in one-to-one situations with children aged between nine and twelve years old. Some had attention deficit disorders and could be awkward at times, but most were well motivated and seemed pleased to see me. When I arrived in the mornings they ran across the playground towards me. Quite uninhibited, they gathered round me like a rugby scrum and hugged me. Life is more informal here, yet they were always respectful.

In addition to my tutoring, Tai, an excellent young teacher I worked with, asked me to introduce some Scottish culture into her class's cultural studies course. A surprising number of Cook Islanders have Scottish ancestors, some of whom may have arrived with the early whalers or traders and jumped ship here - and who could blame them? After many months enduring the privations of life on a sailing ship, Rarotonga must have seemed like paradise with its superb climate, an abundance of food, and beautiful young women. I kept wondering why I didn't stay on myself! Others emigrated to New Zealand as young men, met Cook Island girls working there, and settled on their wives' family land in the islands.

I made my presentation to the class wearing my kilt and taught them some Scottish dances. In the shade of the trees bordering the beach, I walked them through the dances first (I didn't have any music at the time) then clapped my hands to give them the timing. Dancing is important in Polynesian culture. They had a marvellous sense of rhythm, their timing was superb, and they picked it up so quickly. After the music arrived on a CD, there was no holding them back. When I arrived the following morning the entire school was dancing *Strip The Willow* on the playground to the toe-tapping music of the Fergie MacDonald Ceilidh Band. The curiosity of the other classes had been aroused by the sound when we had our first rehearsals with music, and my students had been so keen they had been practising in the playground before school in the morning. The others had all joined in. Imagine - Scottish dance craze sweeps Rarotonga! The teachers were impressed and suggested putting on a display at their prize-giving day. That was something different and earned many favourable comments. I was also honoured by being asked to present the prizes at the ceremony. The kids were cheerful, enthusiastic, and friendly, and it was with considerable sadness that I left at the end of the term.

A few days after I had arrived, a notice of an open seminar at the University of the South Pacific campus on Rarotonga attracted my attention. On Effective Schools, it was led by an American professor, now working in Australia. His thoughts on the subject were aligned with mine and in the open forum I made a short contribution. That prompted several people to speak with me afterwards. One of them, a student teacher who found my words inspiring, suggested I should come to the Teachers' Training College as she felt I had something worth sharing with the students. She introduced me to Teremoana Hodges, the Principal of the Teacher Training College, who was receptive to the idea: "Of course, come and meet the students tomorrow."

Between thirty and forty students had assembled when I arrived. Before we went in to address them Teremoana said, "I don't know enough about you to introduce you. Can you introduce yourself?"

I started by explaining that I had retired as the head of a secondary school, and how I became a world traveller: "My wife died a few years ago, and with no woman to spend all my money for me..." That brought an almighty and joyous chorus.

"We'll help you!"

A rapport had been established and a useful interactive session followed. Most were girls, training for primary education, and afterwards Teremoana introduced me to one of her brightest students, an eighteen year-old girl called Christine from the island of Mangaia. Nearing the end of her first year, she had been selected to represent the Cook Islands at a Commonwealth Youth Conference on Education to be held in Edinburgh the following week. Could I help her in her preparations, brief her on what to expect in Edinburgh, and offer some critical comment on the presentation she was preparing? I was delighted to be asked, and spent some time over the next couple of days with Christine.

She was a good ambassador for the islands. Thoughtful and intelligent, she pulsated with energy and enthusiasm. I felt sure this girl would make an excellent teacher. On her return, she visited me to tell me what a wonderful time she'd had. Wide-eyed with excitement, the words tumbled out. She had been thrilled to be one of a handful of delegates to be invited to lunch with Scotland's then First Minister, Jack McConnell. Her eyes sparkled, "I was amazed. Why me, a girl from the tiny island of Mangaia? No one else there had ever heard of it. In fact, very few had even heard of the Cook Islands. When I went in to the dining room and saw all the silver cutlery on the table, I was terrified. You know, John, in the Cook Islands we normally use our fingers when we eat. That's just our culture." She giggled. "Of course, I know how to use a knife, fork, and spoon, but there were so many of them there. What were they all for? I thought, I'll just wait to see what everyone else does and copy them, and that way I managed to avoid embarrassing myself."

A group of thirty-six Australian student teachers arrived on Rarotonga for one month's teaching practice and the college had planned a day of Cultural Exchange to allow the Cook Island students and the Australians the opportunity to become acquainted, and share aspects of each other's culture. The Cook Islands students wanted me there too, insisting that I wear my kilt, and Teremoana asked me to address the gathering at the start of the day's programme. A Television News crew were present to record the event, and that night a clip of my address to the students appeared on the TV news programme. At the hostel, the backpackers almost choked on their dinners as they recognised the kilted figure on the screen. A spontaneous cheer erupted, followed by cries of, "Hey John, you're on TV! You're a celebrity! Can we have your autograph?"

A few nights later, Chris and Sonne, two Germans from Munich who had just arrived at the hostel, accompanied me to

Banana Court, a popular bar with a dance floor. The Australian students were all there, already dancing, but on spotting the kilt several of the girls rushed over and dragged me on to the floor to dance with them.

The German boys looked on open-mouthed, and when I rejoined them a few minutes later, Chris leaned towards me and said, "John, where can I buy one of these kilts?"

CHAPTER 10

Immaculate Conceptions

My modest degree of celebrity, thanks to the kilt, led to an invitation to lunch with Sir Appenera Short, the former Queen's Representative in the Cook Islands, and his wife, Lady Maui. Lady Maui's great-grandfather was a Scot and she was proud of her Scottish ancestry. Also on the guest list that day was one of the Cook Islands' tribal queens, Mii O'Bryan from Mitiaro (one of the smaller islands), who also happened to be the grandmother of my young friend, the current Miss Tiare, Krystina Kauvai. Mii was delightful company. I loved her mischievous sense of humour and she invited me to visit her on Mitiaro. "Come for at least a week, John - and wear your kilt!"

There were only four of us on the flight to Mitiaro. From the window of the small aircraft, I could see the entire island laid out below me, a small patch of greenery in an infinite ocean. Once an atoll, it had been thrust up out of the ocean and its fossilised coral reefs had been colonised by trees and shrubs. The depression in the centre of the island, formerly a lagoon, now contained a fresh water lake around which a plantation produced fruit and vegetables. The plane dipped its wing, swept low over the reef, and touched down on the crushed coral runway.

I was first off the plane and walked over to the terminal building. No more than an open-sided shelter, it was filled with people, some about to leave the island, others waiting to greet arrivals. I searched the faces. The crowd parted and there was the beaming face of the queen, known to everyone on the island by the endearing title, Aunty Mii. Her arms stretched out in welcome as she greeted me, "Kia Orana, John." She placed an ei (a crown of fragrant flowers) on my head, and another long neck ei on my shoulders. "Come John, and meet the Mamas."

The small shelter was full of ladies all wearing coloured cotton frocks and head eis. First to greet me was her niece, Tungane, whom I had met some weeks earlier on Rarotonga and had danced with her. "Kia Orana, John. Remember me, your dancing partner?" She gave a seductive flick of the hips to remind me.

"Och aye. I'll no' forget *you*!" I assured her. While the introductions went on, one lady led a spontaneous outburst of song, with all the others joining in. The scene now switched from a rather demure gathering into one of outrageous fun as they all swivelled their hips and sang at the top of their voices.

Surrounded by gyrating mamas, the other arrivals smiled, as the attention switched from one to another. It looked rather bawdy to me. It was. The Mitiaro ladies are famed for their bawdy songs.

Standing there bemused, I felt a hand on my knee, stroking the hairs on my leg. The hand belonged to an elderly mama who, with child-like curiosity, was intent on exploring this strange, pale-skinned hairy creature. Maori men don't have hairy legs, so I suppose I did look a bit unusual. And they don't see many kilts on Mitiaro! The hand moved on to feel the texture of my woollen sock, then it began to lift the hem of my kilt.

"Hey, that's private property," I said. She turned her attention to my sporran and began to flick the three tassels on it. A big smile lit up her face, but when Mii turned round and saw what was going on she scolded the woman who scuttled away and was lost in the crowd.

The mamas broke into song again, this time to bid farewell to the lady mayor. Their song was about a centipede trying to crawl up your leg to bite you. One of the mamas started crawling about the floor, acting the part of the centipede, and tried to crawl between the mayor's legs. Her voluminous proportions emphasised the absurdity of her actions, and the long cotton dress the lady mayor was wearing proved an effective barrier to the progress of the 'centipede' into her personal space. The dance finished with a vigorous sideways kick of the leg to thrust the centipede away.

Denied the prize of the lady mayor, it occurred to me that the centipede might seek easier targets. There was a glint in its eye as it moved in my direction. I brought my knees close together in a hurry. I asked Mii if this happened every time a flight came in. She apologised for their uninhibited behaviour, but it was a tradition here. I assured her there was no need for apologies. I had the feeling that my visit to Mitiaro was going to be full of fun.

The lifestyle here was far removed from the relative bustle of Rarotonga. Traditional outrigger canoes lay beached at the tiny inlet that served as a harbour, children played without fear of injury on crushed coral roads, and families of pigs roamed at will. Traffic was conspicuous by its absence: an occasional truck, motorcycle, or the odd bicycle made an appearance from time to time, but it was an occasion when they did. A diesel generator produced electricity for the community, but it was switched off at 10 p.m. There were no pubs, clubs, restaurants, or hotels, and only one small store. Most people now live in modern bungalows, but there are still some of the traditional kikau huts. Visitors to the island are dependent on local families for accommodation.

Rush Hour traffic on Mitiaro

Traditional kikau hut

Being the only tourist on the island, the guest of Aunty Mii - and the only man wearing a kilt - everyone soon knew of me and I was referred to as Papa John, a title that has stuck, and by which I became known thereafter in the Cook Islands. The title 'Papa,' indicative of maturity, or authority, is a mark of respect.

Lunch with Mii consisted of umukai, food cooked in an umu, an earth oven. A fire is set in a hole in the ground and volcanic rocks heaped on the burning timber. When the wood burns down, the rocks retain the heat. Chicken, pork, fish, breadfruit, and taro root are all wrapped in banana leaves and placed on top of the rocks, then covered with more banana leaves, which are then covered with earth. Two hours or so later, the umu (oven) is opened and the kai (food) is taken out. The meat, cooked in its own juices, is tender and succulent with a slight smokey flavour, and is eaten with the fingers. Eating is an important part of the culture here. If you can't eat everything on your plate, your host is likely to clear your leftovers on to his or her plate and finish it for you. Even the fatty or grisly parts I had set aside on the edge of my plate were picked up by Mii and chewed and sucked with relish as she responded to my questions about her role as Ariki, the queen.

Cook Islands society is based on an association to a village and its chief, the Ariki, often referred to as king, or queen. Titles of authority and land rights are passed on through both the male and female lineage. As land cannot be bought or sold, a marriage to someone who has rights to land is of considerable importance. The title of Ariki still carries considerable *mana*, a kind of spiritual power. Respected in their communities, their lifestyle is unpretentious, and they work at everyday jobs. You could find yourself out for a night, having a drink and rubbing shoulders with royalty, as I found out on more than one occasion.

The House of Ariki in the Cook Islands Parliament offers a consultative role in relation to matters of cultural significance and ceremonial affairs.

That night, Tungane joined us for dinner. It proved to be a struggle for me as I had eaten so much at lunchtime. "Come on John, you must eat more," urged Mii. "We'll have to build you up to look like a Cook Island boy." It's not surprising they are big here. There is no shortage of food, but I had been reared on wartime rations and was well and truly stuffed.

The only entertainment on such a small island is what they make for themselves. They like to have a good time, singing and dancing, and are always laughing and joking. Tungane suggested I might teach them some Scottish dances later in the week. "But you had better make sure you wear plenty of layers under your kilt," she added with a serious look on her face. "Oh, these cannibal Cook Island mamas are wild. They'll have no hesitation in sticking their heads up there to see what you're wearing!"

However, it was the week of the government's quarterly inspections of homes. Houses must be clean and habitable, and there must be no pools of standing water outside where mosquitoes might breed. In anticipation of this, all the mamas were busy with their spring cleaning and tidying gardens, so the dancing lesson had to be abandoned.

Mii had arranged for her nephew, Niki, to give me a tour of Mitiaro on his truck. The island is only about eleven miles in circumference, with a circular road and one cross-island road. Niki had left the island as a boy to live in New Zealand with an uncle. He had worked in the food industry, educating himself at the same time. Now in his retirement, he had built a home for himself on the family land with a productive garden around it.

He could catch fish, kill chickens or pigs for meat, and eat his own fresh fruit and vegetables. He needed little else.

He took me to meet his cousin, Marguerite, and her fifteen year-old grandson, Ladislav. I was intrigued by the eastern European name. His late grandfather, a Hungarian, had been Marguerite's husband. Marguerite, now a woman in her fifties, was busy painting her new house. I offered to help, but she was running out of paint. The nearest paint shop was in Rarotonga, so work had to be suspended. Who knows when it will resume? There seemed to be no rush.

That afternoon, I ventured out with my camera and wandered along the shore to the small inlet that served as a landing stage. There are no proper harbours outside Rarotonga. Freight is lowered by derrick from the inter-island cargo ships on to a small barge, which fights its way through the surf to bring the goods ashore. The landing ramp was a poor substitute for a beach, but this was where the children came to swim. It was better than the sharp coral shelf that surrounded the island. I wanted photographs of the island lifestyle, and this was one place to see it.

The kids had no reservations about having their pictures taken, and competed for my attention calling out, "You take smiles of me, Papa John." But when they came out of the water they were stark naked. They had no inhibitions about that either. But what would their parents think if I were to take pictures of them? I explained my predicament later to Mii who laughed, "Oh, that's always been the way of life here. Nobody minds." But I had no doubt about what western society would think if I returned with a digital camera loaded with pictures of naked children.

At 6 a.m. on the Sunday morning I was awakened by the beat of a drum. It was a wake-up call: a few slow beats, alternating with more swift beats. Its persistence and the irregularity of the drum beats defeated the desire to fall asleep again. The church was just a few metres away and this was the signal to allow the villagers time to get dressed for the early morning service. At 7 a.m. the distinctive sound of Cook Islands hymn singing drifted through the morning air: the early morning service had begun. It makes a lot of sense to start early in this climate before the heat of the sun becomes oppressive. I had agreed to attend the later service at 9 a.m. with Mii.

A few moments before nine o'clock, we walked the fifty metres to the church door. The timing was perfect. Everyone else was seated. Mii beckoned me to take a seat on a vacant front pew. Two other village chiefs greeted me with handshakes and the customary "Kia Orana," and took their places on the opposite side of the church. Mii, as befits a queen, made her entrance last and entered her personal box. An elder and the minister also stopped to shake hands and welcome me, before taking seats below the pulpit. The elder had a list of announcements to make which included "...a formal welcome to John, our brother from Scotland. We are pleased you have come to share in our service this morning. We hope you will enjoy your holiday on Mitiaro, and when you return to your homeland we hope you will take with you the abiding love of our people." Later, as he began his sermon, the minister again expressed a personal welcome to me from the pulpit, and offered an apology for the fact that he would be preaching in Maori.

While the offering was being collected, I glanced around behind me. Seated a few feet away were all the children, their brown faces eyeing me with curiosity. From among the pack, one smiling face hissed, "Papa John!" It was one of the small boys I had photographed the evening before. As we made eye contact, he gave me a wink, a dazzling smile, and the thumbs-up sign, as he did when having his picture taken. I grinned and acknowledged his greeting with a wink. A few seconds later, I heard the whisper again, "Papa John." Again the thumbs went up. When it was repeated a third time I felt I had to ignore it as this could go on all through the service. Still, it was good to feel so welcome.

Mitiaro has several limestone caves. With a high water table, most of them are filled with fresh water and are popular for swimming. At the largest cave, the fun-loving local ladies have a tradition of gathering there in late afternoon when the day's work is done, to sing bawdy songs, at the end of which they all plunge into the cooling waters of the pool and have a swim. However, I was denied the opportunity to see this because of the priority given to cleaning the houses prior to inspections.

I went exploring by myself and found the cave. In the shade of the cavern on a hot afternoon, I enjoyed a luxurious swim in its crystal-clear water. It was so transparent that I had to reach down with my finger to locate the surface of the water and make some ripples to judge where it was before diving in. Cool, but not cold, I felt guilty about putting my sweaty body in such pure, clear water.

On my way back, as I passed Marguerite's house, Ladislav spotted me from the passion fruit tree where he was having a snack. He called me over to join him and his two friends, and I spent a pleasant hour talking with the boys. Their interests were fishing, working the plantation, and girls - but there were very few girls on the island. Most girls in their age group had gone to school on Rarotonga, or had started work there. I felt for them; young emerging adult males, laden with testosterone - and the nearest available females were almost two hundred miles away on

Rarotonga. But even there, meeting a girl could be complicated, the boys told me.

Genealogy is very important to Cook Islanders, many of whom can trace their ancestors back to the original tribes who migrated to these islands, but it also has a practical significance. In such small communities the risk of inbreeding is high and many young people have to go abroad to find a partner, another reason why so many Scots seamen were welcomed to these islands, adding new DNA to the gene pool. One of the boys told me, "You've got to know who you are dating. Every time I meet a girl I like, she turns out to be a cousin!"

The term 'cousin' is used to describe anyone with whom you may share a common ancestor. This can be quite complicated as some men father children with two or more women, or a woman may have children by different fathers - and the offspring of such liaisons may not be aware of their blood relatives. Large families are common. Older siblings may leave home to be looked after by a grandparent, for education, or for work. Even in recent times, some fail to keep in touch with their families back home and don't even know their youngest siblings. This can lead to complications when someone turns up a couple of generations later to claim their entitlement to a piece of the family land. Then it is vital to be able to prove your pedigree.

It has long been a tradition in Polynesian society to give children to be brought up by someone else, perhaps a grandparent or an aunt, so they'll have someone to work the plantation, fish for them, and care for them in their old age. A child may be given to a childless couple, so they can have a family to bring up. This still happens. Children are loved in this society, and the giving of a child is regarded as an act of unselfishness, the ultimate gift.

Without formal adoption, children are often brought up within another family, while knowing their true family. They seem quite happy to have two mothers: a feeding mother, the one who looks after them on a day-to-day basis who may be a cousin, an aunt, grandparent, or simply a friend of the parents, while their natural mother may live on another island or work in New Zealand, sending money home to pay for the upkeep of the child. Knowing who your 'cousins' are can be quite a complex business in this society as, in such circumstances, it becomes difficult to distinguish between cousins, brothers and sisters, or just the child next door who may spend more time in your home than in his own. Yet strange as all this may seem to the western mind, it does have advantages. No child is unwanted. Older siblings care for younger ones with obvious enjoyment. To hear a child cry here is a rare event.

Walking back to the village with the boys, we passed a grave, decorated with flowers and other trinkets on a neighbour's land. Even in death, relatives are revered, and it is common to see elaborate, well-tended graves within the family garden. This custom often startles Europeans. Yet why not? The land cannot be sold and remains in the ownership of the family, so ancestors are cared for by future generations. I liked that.

As we entered the village, the boys exchanged some cheerful banter with a pleasant young woman. "Friendly young lady," I remarked as we moved on.

The boys looked at each other and smiled knowingly. "Yes. Friendly." The words were laden with meaning. One of the boys leaned towards me and muttered confidentially. "She's got two kids - and she's still a virgin!"

"Two kids and still a virgin? You mean, the miracle of Immaculate Conception has occurred *twice* here on Mitiaro?"

"Oh!" He doubled up laughing. "I got the wrong word in English. I mean she is still unmarried."

On the final night, with the usual gathering of friends at Mii's house, she made a little speech thanking me for bringing so much laughter to the island. I was touched by that, but had to reply that it was *they* who had made *me* laugh so much.

Next morning, Mii took me to the airport. Already waiting for me were Tungane, Niki, Marguerite, Ladislav and the boys. I was crowned with three head eis, stacked one on top of the other, and two shoulder eis. Smothered in flowers, I was then hugged and kissed by *all* the mamas, some of whom made a real meal of me!

Aunty Mii saying goodbye

CHAPTER 11

Mauke Miracle

From the air, Mauke was another flat island offering glimpses of houses beneath the canopy of trees. The plane skirted the north-west coast and flew past the airstrip. A steep turn took us over the reef and we swooped in over the end of the runway and touched down. A large crowd awaited the arrival of the plane, many of whom were leaving the island after the Christmas holidays to head back to Rarotonga or New Zealand.

Tai, one of the teachers I had worked with at Arorangi primary school, was waiting with a big smile and a head ei for me. She crowned me, with the usual greeting, and introduced me to Ta, my driver, who also had an ei for me. Another young woman came forward. "Kia orana, John. Welcome to Mauke." That was a pleasant surprise. She was one of the students I had addressed in my presentation at the Teachers' Training College.

A wee girl came over to me, looking at the kilt, wide-eyed. "Do you play one of those whistle things?" her fingers making a passable demonstration of bagpipe playing.

"No. I'm sorry I can't play the bagpipes." I said.

"Are you from Rarotonga? I think I've seen you there. My name's Moira. I live at Nikao." Nikao is a village just along the road from Tiare Village where I stayed while on Rarotonga.

A boy about ten years old joined us. "Hey, I saw you in church on Raro."

"How do you know it was me?"

"You were wearing that skirt thing," he replied, pointing to the kilt. I could never fool an identity parade here.

Two teenage boys, hovering nearby, approached me. "Hi. Do you live on Raro?"

"Well, yes, I have been there for a few months."

"Do you know a girl called Moira?"

"Moira George?" Moira was Tai's younger sister.

"That's right. She's our cousin. We met you on Raro a few weeks ago." I remembered then. I'd met Moira with her cousins on a Saturday evening and she had introduced me to them.

And I thought no one knew me on this island, apart from Tai!

Ta, a sturdy, athletic looking man in his forties with the build of a rugby player took me in an old, open-top landrover to meet the family. His wife was a teacher and her parents, Tau and Kuru, were retired teachers. They kept a few chalets for visitors and provided all the meals. Tau had also been a headmaster, so we had much in common. He'd worked on several of the islands, but he'd retired to his family land on Mauke, where he'd been the Government Representative for several years. They offered me the use of an ancient bicycle, of 1930s vintage I would guess. It was very low geared and had a maximum speed of about five miles per hour, but it allowed me to explore the island comfortably and visit one of its peculiarities.

On an elevated site between the two villages in the centre of the island, the missionaries built a church in the nineteenth century. Though large enough to accommodate all the worshipers from both villages, the people of the two villages could not come to an agreement on the interior décor, so each half was decorated according to the wishes of the respective factions. The pulpit is situated centrally, with the people from each village sitting in the pews on either side. They even have separate doors. United in faith they may be, but the old tribal traditions and rivalries still simmer under the veneer of Christianity.

Mauke Church, two gateways and two doors

In the afternoon, I cycled down to the tiny harbour. Hordes of kids were having boisterous fun: plunging in off the quay, swimming, throwing each other in, boogie boarding on the surf that surged through the narrow entrance in the reef. The place was pulsating with activity and I couldn't help being infected by their enthusiasm. I pulled off my shirt and strolled on to the quay. Moira, the wee girl I'd met at the airport, came over to advise me that the water was deep all alongside the quay, so I could dive in anywhere. I did, and she jumped in beside me intent on continuing our conversation as we swam back to the shore. She fired questions at me in rapid succession: "What is your name? What is your Mum's name? What is your Dad's name? How old are you?"

Wee Moira, my personal assistant

As we reached the shallows, I turned to face her and the sunlight shone directly on my face. She gasped in amazement, came closer and peered into my eyes. "Your eyes are blue! I've never seen blue eyes before."

That surprised me, but it shouldn't have. The Cook Islanders have brown eyes and I explained that blue eyes were common in my country. I climbed out and dried myself off, but I couldn't shake wee Moira off. She had appointed herself to the role of personal assistant, introducing me to everyone else. When I took my camera out, she organised groups of young posers, all of whom were keen to have their picture taken and they giggled with delight when they saw the results on the camera. Everyone there now knew me, thanks to Moira. She was eight years old.

A teenage girl then came over. She smiled at me as though she had known me for years and said, "Hello. When did you get here? Did you come over from Mitiaro?"

"No. From Rarotonga. But how did you know I was on Mitiaro?"

"You were on Mitiaro just before Christmas. You were staying with Aunty Mii, weren't you? I was there visiting my cousin. You came and spoke with a group of us playing volleyball one night."

I shook my head in amazement and laughed. Here I was on a tiny island with only about three hundred people living on it, about one hundred and seventy miles out in the ocean from Rarotonga, and it was infested with people who knew me. It brought home to me just how small a community the Cook Islands is, despite the considerable distances between the islands. The concept of neighbourhood is different here. It is impossible to remain incognito.

We traded names. Her name was also Moira. I remarked on how many girls seemed to be named Moira on this island. She laughed. "Yes, it's a very common name here. We had a Scottish doctor here called Archie Geanies. He died a few years ago. He was a real character and very popular with everyone on the island and his wife's name was Moira. He delivered all the babies on the island for about thirty years, and just about every family named one of the baby girls after his wife."

"Ah, that explains it. So Moira George would have been one of the babies he delivered?"

"That's right. You know Moira?"

I explained I had worked with Tai and met Moira through her. "You'll know the family no doubt," I added.

"Oh yes," and she then rattled off a seemingly endless list of all their names. I was amazed.

"That's some size of a family. How many are there?"

"Twelve. That's quite common here. There are lots of big families, especially among the Catholics."

Sixteen years old, this girl attended school on Rarotonga, lived there with her aunt, and was home in Mauke for Christmas. She left me then to join some friends. "Have a nice holiday. I'll see you again."

I had no doubt that would be true. After she had gone, a portly middle-aged man drying himself with his towel approached me and introduced himself. He was the local minister and, like all the others, his curiosity was aroused. We spent several minutes in conversation. When I left, he invited me to drop in on him anytime for a chat. Mauke was proving to be a sociable place.

"Here John, try this," said Tau passing me a local delicacy, a sun-dried banana. I'd never seen a dried banana before. About the size of a large date and of similar texture, it was very tasty, all the flavour having been concentrated in the shrivelled flesh, and it was only about one sixth of its original size. He took me outside to show me how it is done. The bananas are split and laid out on a white corrugated iron, or plastic, sheet in the sun and covered with mosquito netting to keep the flies off. Turned daily for the next five days, they shrivel and become a rich brown in colour. They are then wrapped up in dried pandanus leaves and tied tightly, each bundle weighing about 1kg. Hung up in a dry place, they will keep for years. He sold his dried bananas to retailers in Rarotonga. Thus preserved, there is no problem waiting for a ship to freight them off, and he got a good price for them.

Drying bananas

They have such an abundance of food. Breadfruit, boiled or fried, and served as an accompaniment to roast chicken, pork or fish, is delicious. And it can be made into a sweet pudding. Tomatoes grow in profusion. They have taro root and taro leaves, arrowroot, tapioca, pineapples, limes, bananas, passion fruit, and the paw paw (papaya) trees produce fruit all the year round. Goats and pigs graze in the bush, fish are plentiful around the shores, and coconut trees are everywhere. It's easy to understand why so many people return to the islands and retire to a life of plenty. It is impossible to starve here.

Tau, now in his late seventies, was only fit for light duties and the work in the plantation was left to Ta. On a small island like this with such a limited market for fresh produce, the community works together to ensure that everyone has a share of the market. Each year it is decided who should grow each crop rather than have a free for all, which could result in a surplus of one crop and a shortage of another. The crops are rotated among the growers, so that everyone has some income. It is very civilised: a nice kind of 'communism.'

Another treat came my way at lunchtime. Kuru had prepared some uti, the scraped out contents of a sprouted coconut. It was delicious. No matter what age a coconut is, it can be used. The young green nuts are perfect for drinking, as they are full of liquid. The mature brown nuts have plenty of flesh for eating; the flesh can also be grated and squeezed through a muslin cloth, or traditionally through a handful of fine grass, to produce coconut cream which is used in cooking. Even after the coconut has sprouted, there is still good eating in it. The flesh is soft and rich in sugar, and it makes the most delicious and refreshing thick drink with a sprinkling of lime juice. Accompanied by cabin bread, broken up and soaked in it, it made a substantial lunch- time snack. I had no need for anything more.

After lunch, Kura introduced me to some bush medicine. She had fallen off her motorbike and her foot was bruised and swollen. She showed me how to make a poultice of crushed leaves to take away the swelling on her ankle. Using a wooden bowl as a mortar, with a pestle fashioned from volcanic rock, she crushed a bundle of leaves Tau had gathered that morning. When the leaves had been crushed into a dark green mush, she added some coconut oil and a selection of herbs, blended it all together, and wrapped it in a cloth. It was then wrapped around her foot and tied at the ankle. This medication is known as Mauke Miracle.

Some years back, a Mauke woman had a dream in which she was given the recipe for mixing certain herbs with coconut oil as a treatment for injuries. When she woke up, she went out to seek the plants required, mixed the recipe according to her dream, and she had a medicine with amazing properties for removing pain and swelling. Word soon got about and an American who owned a perfume factory on Rarotonga saw its potential and marketed it under the name, Mauke Miracle. I suspect that the key ingredient was the same plant that Kanai had wrapped my leg in the year before, when I had broken my Achilles Tendon in Fiji. That treatment had allowed me to move on to Australia: to travel through Victoria, New South Wales, and Queensland, and do my Advanced Diver's Course on the Great Barrier Reef, before coming home to Scotland for surgery!

With three flights per week to Muake from Rarotonga, the arrival of the plane is a major event in the otherwise sleepy life of the island. Like many others, I went along to watch its arrival. The airfield was teaming with folk, and once more my youthful friends greeted me. A small amount of cargo, mostly food and provisions for the three small general stores, was heaped on to a couple of trucks with a handful of teenagers piled on top to keep it all aboard. With so many people leaving their relatives on the island after the Christmas holiday to return to their homes in Rarotonga, Australia, or New Zealand, tears flowed. One woman had so many friends and relatives to say goodbye to that the plane's departure was delayed to allow her to get round them all. This was a civilised way of life. People came first.

When the plane had taken off, the airstrip emptied. I lingered a few minutes, reflecting on all I had witnessed: the hustle and bustle of people and goods coming and going, the gleeful greetings, the poignant partings. For some elderly people, this might be the last time they would see the island of their birth.

It was all familiar. I had often witnessed the same comings and goings, the excitement, the news-gathering, and the sadness as the ferries sailed from the islands of Scotland. They provided brief interludes of interest, anticipation, and activity in the quiet lives of the islanders.

When they had all gone, the island dozed in the sun once more. I listened to the muffled heartbeat of the ocean as the surf pounded out on the reef, and to the gentle breathing of the island as the wind sighed among the palm fronds. Here was peace.

That evening, I returned to the harbour to watch the fun again. A big swell thundered on the reef, and I watched in amazement as the kids sat on the edge of the jetty to get battered by the huge waves that broke right over it. The concrete surface of the jetty, almost always wet with spray, was covered in slippery algae. As the big waves erupted over the jetty, they struck the children on their backs and scattered them across the slippery surface. They insisted I join them. Wee Moira grabbed me by the hand and led me over to the edge. "Come on, Papa John. It's great fun. You'll love it."

Waiting for the wave

Scattered by the wave

I reflected for a moment as I sat there waiting for the next big wave. Here I was, a pensioner, sitting half-naked among all these kids aged from about five to sixteen, waiting to have my back pounded by tons of cascading seawater. An excited cry went up.

"Another big one!"

An intense thump, the jetty trembled, and a wall of water erupted skywards. Then it fell and hit us. It was like being struck by a huge bat and I was shooting across the surface of the jetty on my backside towards the rock wall at the landward end. I stopped a few feet short, dripping wet. Wee Moira was right. It *was* good fun. I rushed back to the edge to rejoin the kids, to be thumped on the back by the next big wave.

At the church service on the Sunday, I took my seat in the neutral pews in the centre, facing the pulpit, with the villagers segregated on either side of me according to the village and tribe they belonged to. As on Mitiaro, I received a personal welcome from the pulpit, and after the service the minister invited me to join him for lime juice and biscuits. He had been born on Penrhyn, the most northerly of the Cook Islands, and had served as a minister on several islands. Making shell jewellery was his hobby and he presented me with a Maori fishhook necklet, a distinctive, traditional shape carved from a piece of shell. He urged me to stay on the island and apply for a teaching post.

"Please give it some thought, John. We are desperately short of good teachers. You are the kind of person we need here. I can see it by the way you relate to the kids, and how they all flock round you. Why don't you try it for a year?"

It was tempting. I had developed a fondness for this island and its people, the fifth Cook Island I had visited, but I had the same feeling about all the other islands. The prospect of living the life of an islander for a whole year appealed to me. Everyone on the island knew me now. They all waved and called out to me on passing. It would be interesting to stay longer, become an active member of the community. I could absorb the culture and learn the language. But tying myself to a contract for a year? Since retiring, I had enjoyed freedom of movement to visit countries I had only dreamed about before. There would be the marking of exercises, the necessary preparation, the inevitable paperwork, all of which I had been glad to leave behind. And I had my boat in Scotland for sailing in the summer. I had my family there. I found it hard to sacrifice all that.

I had to leave the island the next day. After I checked in my luggage I turned around and there, waiting behind me with big grins on their faces, were several of the boys from the harbour ready to shake my hand and see me off. More of the kids arrived, and said their goodbyes. Wee Moira assured me she would see me on Rarotonga. A few other people came across to wish me well. At the last moment the minister's wife arrived, apologising for her husband's absence due to duty, and rushed over to give me a hug.

I walked out to the plane, turned, and gave them all a wave. Hands were raised in reply and cries of "Bye, Papa John" echoed in my ears as I climbed the steps to take my seat.

I liked Mauke.

CHAPTER 12

Duties of Papa John

While you might get the impression that life is one big holiday for me, the title Papa John does not come without responsibilities.

Nikki, a vivacious Scottish girl, who'd stayed a few days at Tiare Village, had a young Uruguayan accountant escorting her. She introduced us one evening and then went off to the ladies room. That was the cue for some man talk. Later, she engineered some time alone with me and told me she loved his Latin-American charm, especially the accent, but she also had a promising romantic interest in the USA, where she worked for a travel company. However, right now she was still unattached, she was on holiday, and she had this handsome young Latino panting after her. She needed a sounding board, someone older to talk with, a father figure - and Papa John was the obvious choice. She asked me what I thought. The boy seemed decent enough to me, but she would have to make her own decisions as to how she should proceed, and I added, "I suppose I might allow you snog him."

She beamed. "Thanks, Papa John. You're a real gent."

Nikki had to move from Tiare Village to another hostel because of prior bookings and a few days later we met outside the internet café. She was climbing on to her scooter with her back to me as I pulled in behind her. "I'd ken these legs anywhere." I growled.

She spun round and laughed, "Oh, whit are ye like?" We went into a café and had a chat. On her way home to Scotland, it was to be her last night on the island, and she wanted to see me on her final night out. It would be a shame to disappoint the girl so, in the call of duty, I was out again that night with Lars, a young German who shared a chalet with me, to 'see her off' at Banana Court.

Lars headed to the bar to buy the drinks while I was distracted by two young Cook Island ladies who admired the kilt. At least, I presume, in my modesty, that it was the kilt and not the man in it that excited their attention - but of course I could be wrong.

Conversation came easily, and a little of the Maori tongue eased things along even better. They were surprised we had never met before, but they were both married. One of them, Tanya, was secretary to the owner of The Flame Tree Restaurant, one of Rarotonga's most prestigious, and she expressed surprise that I'd never eaten there. "Now this won't do. You must come round some night. Just phone up and ask for me, and I'll arrange it all for you."

"To eat in a place like that I'd need to have the right company," I protested. "I wouldn't want to eat out alone. Lars there is alright to go out with for a couple of beers, but for the Flame Tree I'd want to have a charming female companion to dine with."

She waved her hand around and said, "Well, what's stopping you? There are plenty of beautiful girls here." There was no denying that.

A few minutes later, I joined Nikki and a few other friends for her farewell bash. She introduced me to Leanne who'd just arrived that day. She was staying in the same hostel as Nikki on the other side of the island, but now found herself in an unfortunate situation. However, Nikki came to the rescue.

"Leanne is going to be the only girl left in the hostel in a couple of days time. There will only be her and a Norwegian honeymoon couple so she'll have no one to go out with, but I told her not to worry, Papa John would look after her."

See what I mean? The responsibilities just keep piling up.

Attractive, intelligent, and instantly likeable (I mean Leanne, not Papa John) I felt sure that the execution of my new responsibility would be a pleasure rather than a burden. I wasted no time.

"Have you anything planned at all?"

"No."

"Okay, on Thursday nights I organise a table at the Staircase Restaurant for people from Tiare Village for the Island Night Show. It's a chance to see some traditional dancing. Interested in joining us?"

Nikki chipped in with some encouragement, having been one of those I had taken the previous week. Leanne, smiling, said, "Okay, count me in."

"Now on Friday night I suggest dinner at the Flame Tree Restaurant. I've just been scolded by the owner's secretary for never having eaten there, but I need someone to dine with me."

Again, Nikki chipped in with support. She had dined there a few days ago.

Leanne beamed. "Sounds great."

Nikki beamed too, "See, I told you Papa John would take good care of you."

Leanne grinned. "This is fantastic. I only arrived this morning, didn't know anyone, and now all this is happening to me. I can't believe it."

I went to the toilet. On my way back, I passed Tanya. "Tanya, I've taken your advice and found myself a beautiful young lady to dine with. When you go into the office tomorrow, please make a reservation for Friday night at 7:30 for a table for two." She looked at me in amazement.

"Wow! That didn't take you long! How did you manage that?"

I shrugged. "The kilt and the Scottish accent?"

At the Island Night Show we had a table fronting the dance floor. In his welcome to the guests, the leading male 'warrior' prances about and appears to shout aggressively at you, but it is all quite amicable. He approached Leanne, bent on one knee before her, looked into her eyes, kissed her hand, and uttered a few quiet words with a mischievous twinkle in his eye. I was sure he would be back later. I was right.

At one point, he demonstrated husking a coconut with his bare teeth, an astonishing feat. He chose Leanne to demonstrate cracking the nut open with a drum stick. This can be done with one strike by a skilled practitioner, but with Leanne he pretended she had hit his hand as she delivered a blow that failed to make any impression on the nut. He then finished the job himself, cracking the nut neatly in two. Again bending on one knee before her, he offered her one half of the nut from which to drink the juice, keeping the other to himself. Then, linking his drinking arm with hers, he drew her towards him and they drank, arms linked in romantic style.

She was now a star, but more was yet to come. In the final dance, the Ura Peani (the European's dance, a clever play on the words Ura, meaning dance, and European), in which the tourists are invited to dance with the experts, she was again first to be picked - but not by the alpha male this time. One of the younger boys in the dance team had his wits about him and made a dash for her, getting in before the alpha male, much to his chagrin and everyone's amusement. After the show, Tere and some of the local boys joined us again for the regular dancing and Leanne was never short of partners from among the local boys.

Dinner at the Flame Tree was a mouth-watering experience and afterwards Leanne was interested in seeing the nightlife of Rarotonga, so I took her on the motorbike to Avarua, where it all happens. We stopped off first at the Cocobar to give her a glimpse of local colour. Tere and the local lads were there and greeted us. They were bound for Banana Court, so we followed a few minutes later.

It was there that a whirlwind arrived in the shape of Junior - a big Maori rugby player, then playing as a professional in Australia. Born in New Zealand of Cook Island parents, he was a nephew of Adrienne's, the hostel manager. I was talking with Leanne when I spotted his face in the crowd. Thrusting people aside, he made a beeline for me.

"Papa John!" he exploded – Junior doesn't do things by half – and then he smothered me in a bear hug. "Papa John, it is so good to see you again."

"Aye, good to see you too, big fella," I gasped from somewhere under his armpit. He was over for the International Rugby Sevens Tournament. Also in his wake came his cousin, Nancy, Adrienne's daughter, who had recently returned home after two years working in Brussels.

I had met Junior the previous year at Christmas when he and I had enjoyed some memorable bonding moments. Having imbibed a little too much Christmas spirit on Christmas Eve, he got a wee bit out of hand. He was all over the place, greeting everyone with cries of 'Merry Christmas,' wandering on to the middle of the road to ensure that those in cars did not miss their share of his Christmas goodwill, but coming close to ensuring that it would be his last if someone didn't rein him in. Nancy had promised to get him home safely, but he was proving to be too much of a handful and would not do as he was told. She was then verging on tears, so wild and erratic was his behaviour. I told her to leave him to me, that I would see him home. A little assertive diplomacy was required.

Grabbing him by the shirt collar and drawing him down to my height, I growled a few caring words into his face. It had the desired effect, and he ended up draped over my shoulder as I dragged him home. I tuck in neatly under his armpit.

He kept on muttering, "Papa John, I'll do anything you say. I respect you Papa John. Papa John, Aunty Adrienne doesn't need to know a word of this." And when I assured him my lips were sealed if he behaved himself and went to bed, he said, "I'll be good, Papa John. I promise you. I respect you, Papa John." When I left him at his chalet he called out, "Papa John, you're one cool guy."

I smiled. "Yeah, cool." The absurdity of it all amused me.

Now, a year later, he was back among us creating more mayhem. With Junior and the rest of the rugby boys, plus Tere and the local lads all joining us, Leanne was never short of company and we had the ingredients of a really good party.

Leanne was keen to do the cross-island trek, so I led her across the island on the Sunday afternoon. I was now Papa John - jungle guide. We made good time to The Needle, a pinnacle rising from the central volcanic ridge. After a rest there, we dropped down through the rainforest with its giant ferns to the waterfall at the far side of the island. I pulled off my boots and shirt and plunged into the cool refreshing water beneath the falls. Leanne slipped off her outer layer to reveal a bikini, all in place and ready for action, and she joined me in the pool.

The Needle

Whigmore's Waterfall

On returning to my chalet, I got busy in the kitchen. I was now Papa John, chef. While preparing dinner, with Lars assisting, Volker, another German from the next chalet, dropped in and I invited him to join us, so we had four for dinner. The conversation never flagged, with plenty of laughter until 11:30 p.m. when I had to drive Leanne back home. Papa John - chauffeur.

The following day, Leanne was leaving for a few days on Aitutaki. On the day she returned, she had twelve hours to wait for her flight back to England, so Lars and I offered her the use of our chalet to rest and have something to eat before her flight. I then took her to the airport. I felt I had executed my various duties as Papa John in a fitting manner. Leanne seemed to think so too. We exchanged email addresses and she came with a friend to sail with me in Scotland the following summer. Papa John - yacht captain. It's a demanding life being Papa John.

CHAPTER 13

Unexpected Events

A traditional dance team from the small, northern island of Rakahanga had won first place in the National Dance Competitions and were putting on a performance at Banana Court. A good crowd had assembled, including the visiting rugby players taking part in the international sevens tournament. The dance team put on a good show and, as usual, some of the audience were invited to dance with them. After the guests had done their bit, the compere asked if there were any others in the audience who wanted to try some Cook Island dancing.

No one volunteered. He cast his eye around the crowd. His gaze stopped at me.

"Hey, there's a Scottish man wearing a kilt! Why didn't you get picked to dance, sir?" I shook my head and shrugged.

"Well, let's put that right. Would you care to join us for some Cook Island dancing now, sir?"

Hungry for the sight of a kilt swinging to the primitive drumbeat of Maori music, the rugby boys cheered me on. It would be a shame to disappoint them. I walked on to the dance floor.

"Now sir, first of all, greet your partner and say 'Kia Orana'," called out the compere. I knew the form. Most people shake hands with the partner and give a brief peck on the cheek - but I'd done this before.

Coming from one of the most northerly islands, this dance team didn't know me. And if they were going to have some entertainment at my expense, then I was taking all the perks going. Instead of the usual timid tourist tickle of lips on cheek and handshake at five paces, I stepped forward like a true warrior and wrapped my arms around the girl. Call me insatiable if you like, but at my stage in life you don't get that many chances, and I need to make the most of every opportunity.

The girl played along beautifully - they just need a hint of encouragement. Her eyes flashed with a look of ecstasy / desire / passion / lust - just pick a word, any one will do. She eagerly responded to my embrace and wrapped her arms around me. I waggled my rear end and swung my kilt to show how much I was enjoying myself, the girl giggled with delight, and the crowd roared. So too, did the compere.

"Hey Papa! Get your hands off! That's my wife!" The crowd laughed again. I released her, flicked my eyebrows, and smiled at her. Her eyebrows flicked up too and she smiled back. Affirmative: she'd enjoyed it as much as I had.

Then the drums started to beat. The girl said, "Just knock your knees together like this," and gave a weak impression of the male dance. She had no idea I had rehearsed with one of the professional dance teams in Avarua.

"Och hen, I can dae better than that," I retorted and launched into a vigorous impression of Maori warrior dancing. I began to circle her, knees oscillating rapidly, enclosing her within my outstretched arms and hands, which were making all sorts of gestures, each one suggestive of something - and whatever it was, her eyes opened wide in wonder.

"Hey, that's great!" She launched herself into the female part, hips making like a washing machine, hands and arms telling their story in response to mine, her gyrating body snaking within my arms in a seductive manner. The audience loved it and cheered, but I was concentrating on the drumbeats. I had to synchronise the ending in time with the last drumbeat, just as the pros do. I once saw a professional dancer execute a marvellous ending in which he whipped the girl off her feet and sat her on his bended knee in perfect time with the final drumbeat. That was too optimistic for me, but recognising the final few beats, I raised myself from the almost crouching warrior position, threw my arms open wide again and stepped forward one pace. The girl read the gesture and stepped into my embrace, wrapping her arms around me in a flamboyant gesture. My arms closed around her and I planted a kiss on her cheek right on the final beat of the drum. The crowd erupted. It was, in Cook Island dancing, my finest hour.

I released her and she grinned at me. "That was fantastic!"

"Aye, you were no' bad either," I replied with typical Scottish understatement. The generosity of my rustic compliment quite overwhelmed her and, swept away on a tide of euphoria, she drew me to her bosom again. I savoured her embrace for a few lingering moments. The compere could shout as much as he liked. I reckon I had earned it.

Sapna, an Indian girl, born and brought up in England, was one of the backpackers at the hostel. She had never ridden a motorcycle before and was worried about taking the hired bike out on the road for the first time. I took her to the market place, now deserted as it was a public holiday, to give her some experience in handling the motorbike away from the road and we embarked on a trip round the island to build up her confidence. We stopped to have a look at the Nuku, the colourful pageant commemorating the arrival of Christianity to the islands. It was a big occasion, so I was wearing my kilt. Afterwards, we drove round the island stopping at the waterfall, a popular scenic spot. Sitting at a picnic table, a couple of middle-aged ladies and some young people in their early twenties were tucking into some food. The unexpected sight of a kilt attracted their attention and we were called over.

Nuku Pageant

"Please, come and share in our picnic."

Sapna whispered, "Oh, we can't."

"Hospitality is part of the culture here. We don't need to take much, but it would be offensive if we didn't join them."

We sat with them and took a little of their food. Introductions over, the questions flowed to satisfy their curiosity. On hearing that I had been here before, they asked if I knew anyone on this side of the island. When I mentioned Krystina, who held the Miss

Tiare title at the time, they smiled in recognition. "Krystina is my niece," said Mata, one of the women, "and these are her cousins. Her father is my brother."

As we talked, the cousins went swimming in the pool below the falls. No one here seems to change into swimwear. They go in fully clothed and sit in the sun afterwards to dry out. I would have loved to join them, but a waterlogged kilt didn't appeal too much.

After the swimming, the conversation drifted to our respective traditions in music and dancing. Sapna was asked to demonstrate a traditional Indian dance, I did some Scottish Highland Dancing, and they taught us how to dance Cook Islands style. The table became an improvised drum with Mata and her sister beating out the rhythm. The young ones all joined in, dancing in all three styles. The picnic had become a party, and the party then became an event imprinted in my mind forever as Tara, a vivacious girl who worked as a flight attendant with Air Rarotonga, began to sing. Her dark hair glistened, still wet from swimming; her damp clothes stuck to her body, her smile was soft and serene, and she had the voice of an angel. A gentle song of love filled the air in that lush, green, jungle amphitheatre with the waterfall whispering in the background. As the final notes of the song drifted away in the mellow evening air, the sun slipped behind the trees, bringing the day to a memorable end.

For relaxation at the end of a day's work, a bit of snorkelling or swimming in the warm water of the lagoon is one of the delights of life on a tropical island. Sheltered by the reef from the big Pacific breakers which thunder on to it, the lagoon, with its incredible pale turquoise colour, invites you to cool off when the afternoon sun has lost some of its intensity. You don't have to swim or snorkel.

Many of the locals prefer to sit fully clothed in water about two feet deep, chatting with friends and neighbours.

One afternoon, I had snorkelled across the lagoon to the reef to explore the coral and observe the multi-coloured fish which live there. On my return, the shore line was busy with mamas and children, free from school. As I surfaced near the water's edge and removed my mask, I was now recognisable and a cry erupted from a few yards away.

"Papa John!" A group of kids from the school were running towards me and threw themselves into the water beside me. "Papa John, let me try your mask," cried one, and then they all had to have a go. Some wanted me to throw them over my shoulder into the water, the young ones wanted me to put on the mask and snorkel, pretending to be a shark chasing them through the shallows.

The idea of a quiet, reflective dip in the lagoon had evaporated. It was now Playtime with Papa John. One of the mothers who knew me came over and relaxed in the water, chatting with me as though we were lounging on chairs on a veranda.

As most of them left to go home, the mother who knew me waded out to the reef now that the tide was low to gather maturori, the roe of the sea cucumber. Few things in the sea look less appetising than a sea cucumber. Like a fat sausage, anything from a few inches to a foot or more in length, its skin has the texture of canvas. They are found in great profusion here, lying on the lagoon bottom or on the reef, sifting through the sand. Holding each sea cucumber, head up, she made a small incision with her knife on its flank and the roe spurted out of the slit she had made. It looks like fine spaghetti with a slightly pink hue, and as she squeezed the sea cucumber's sides it all flowed out. I held a plastic box to catch the roe and she tossed the sea cucumber into the water again. They seem to suffer no harm from this incision.

They soon patch up the slit and produce more roe, which can be harvested again and again. It is usually eaten raw, sometimes fried, and has a shrimp-like flavour.

There were plenty of sea urchins too, clinging to holes in the coral. "Ever eaten one of these before?"

I shook my head. She stripped the spines off one, sliced her knife through it, and pulled out some gelatinous mess, leaving some light brown muscle tissue in the shape of a five-pointed star exposed on the curved wall of the urchin.

"That's the bit you eat," she told me, scraping the muscle away from the shell with her knife. She then held the knife to my lips for me to suck off the meat. Well, I thought, it's the way the Polynesians have survived for centuries so it's unlikely to do me any harm. I opened my mouth and accepted the morsels she offered me. Quite pleasant, with the fresh salty flavour of the sea, it would serve as a starter. There were also some black sea urchins, very striking looking, and she told me to try one of them as they taste different. This time there was more muscle to be had, but it was of a more gelatinous consistency. She scraped it all to the bottom of the shell and then told me to drink it. I was surprised at its sweet taste - a sort of seafood dessert.

I'd had my starter and dessert, but now I was hungering for my dinner. As we made our way back to the shore, I cast my eye around. The surface of the lagoon was now a burnished gold, reflecting the rays of the dying sun. The coral heads protruded from the water at low tide, and much of the reef was exposed, a dark rampart against the thrusting ocean outside.

All along the reef were the huddled figures of people, silhouetted against the setting sun. It was a picture of life being lived in timeless fashion; people out on the reef, harvesting the sea as their ancestors had done for thousands of years.

New Year's day was quiet, but in the evening a couple of the lads came out with me to see if anything was happening in town. We drove our motorbikes into the Island Bar car park. A police car that had been parked at the roadside had followed us, coming to a halt between me and the boys.

"Happy New Year, Papa John!" It was Nane, one of the local female police constables. "Hey, when are you leaving?"

"Next Saturday."

"Oooooh. I'm gonna miss seeing that kilt around the island. Can I have your email address, Papa John. I'd love to keep in touch with you."

"Aye, sure. Have you a pen and some paper?"

"Tell you what, I'll give you mine and you can then email me and I'll get yours that way." She picked up a notepad and began writing her address for me. At that point the boys came round to see what was happening.

Noticing her scribbling on her pad, one of the boys asked "Are you getting booked? What have you done?"

I laughed. "No. She's giving me her address and telephone number." I flashed the piece of paper at him.

As things were quiet on the crime front, Nane chatted with us for a while. "Okay boys, I've got to go now and look for drunk drivers." She nodded in the direction of the Island Bar: "Have a good time, but be careful. If I see you coming, I'll make sure I'm looking the other way." And with a wave she drove off.

The boys stared after her in disbelief. "Would you believe it? What a civilised police force."

CHAPTER 14

Intimate Encounter

Our final stop on any night out was the Cocobar, which was on the way back to the hostel. Frequented mostly by Cook Islanders, it was a bit rough and ready, but had a welcoming atmosphere and when someone dragged me on to the dance floor, the music inspired me to introduce some Cook Island dance movements in my repertoire. This attracted the attention of a party of ten young ladies who were having a girls' night out and they joined in, sidling up closer, arms flowing in movements of poetic grace, hips swaying sensuously. One girl danced round behind me, began rubbing her posterior against mine, and we boogied back-to-back. The others enclosed us in the centre of a circle, cheering, and whooping with delight.

Those who know how shy and withdrawn I am in the social scene back home (I know you won't believe me, but it's true!) may well raise eyebrows at this ostentatious display of erotic dancing, but the primitive beat of the drum overpowered the thin veneer of Western culture. And when you're caught in the tide, you just have to go with the flow.

As we made our way out to go home, the girls were leaving too and a couple of them stopped to talk, telling me they had Scottish ancestors. It seemed an appropriate time for introductions.

"Ko'ai to'ou ingoa?" I asked. (What is your name?)

"Ko Moana to'ou ingoa. (My name is Moana) Ko'ai to'ou ingoa?" (What is your name?)

"Ko Hoani to'ou ingoa." (My name is Hoani = Johnnie)

"Hey, that's really cool! You speak our language!" Moana beamed and wrapped her arms around me. A wee bit of the local language, spoken with a Scottish accent while wearing the kilt, seemed to have an aphrodisiacal effect!

Another girl joined us and asked the usual question about what is worn under the kilt. Moana was horrified, shooed her away, and apologised for her shocking behaviour. Concerned that I might have been offended by such a rude question, she was overwhelmed by a need to console me and hugged me yet again. And I could find no reason whatsoever to dissuade her. I was quite happy to assume some semblance of offence. The silken touch of her cheek caressing mine was indeed very soothing. She murmured abject apologies while holding me close and I reassured her, my lips flicking sensuously against her ear. Then, as the girls all climbed on to their small motorbikes, the usual form of transport here, they called me over for one final hug each before they left.

The second from last, the one who had asked me the 'rude' question earlier, was very pretty and instead of giving me the usual hug she reached out her right hand, took mine and drew me towards her. She raised her left hand, placed it round my neck, drew my face down to hers, and kissed me full on the lips. And this wasn't just a peck! She lingered awhile. Of course it would have been ungentlemanly of me to have recoiled from her embrace. You've got to go with the flow. Maybe she was just trying to make amends for 'offending' me earlier. Having released me with a longing look, (well, it looked longing to me!) I turned to Moana who was last in the queue to say goodnight.

Whether inspired by what she had seen, or whether she was determined to claim territorial rights, I don't know, but she too raised her lips to mine and gave me an even more lingering goodnight kiss. Such was the quality, intensity, and longevity of her performance that the other girls all cheered. I would have cheered too had I not been – and I modestly admit to it – an inspirational part of the performance.

It had been a very long time since I had last exchanged lingering good-night kisses with a pretty girl, but as with city buses, two came along at once. It's great what wearing a kilt can do for you!

You may wonder, after such a promising encounter, what happened next? A few days later, I dropped in to the Cocobar again. As I waited to be served at the bar, I glanced around and my eyes met those of one of the girls who had been dancing with me that night. Her eyes lit up. "John! How nice to see you again." Then she turned and beckoned to another young lady sitting with her back to us talking to a man. "Do you remember my friend?"

I looked at the back of the girl's head, then moved a little to the side. "It's Moana."

"That's right. Do you remember her?" She had a mischievous glint in her eye.

I drew her a look. "I'll never forget her!"

She laughed, then reached out to touch Moana on the shoulder. "Hey Moana, look who's here." Moana turned, her eyes opened wide, but with a look of sheer panic.

"Oh my God!" She muttered and turned away rapidly. I thought she was just a bit embarrassed, the shock of coming face to face with me again after our session of prolonged osculatory pleasure.

I sought to put her at ease and said, "Nice to see you again, Moana. How are you tonight?"

She turned again. Anguish was written all over her face. With a look of desperate pleading, she waved her hand in the direction of her male companion. "John, meet my husband!" I almost burst out laughing, but played it cool and held out my hand.

"Hello. Nice to meet you."

"Hey, you're Scottish!" His eyes glowed as he took in the kilt and we spent a few moments chatting about it, a useful diversion, for poor Moana was in an agony of embarrassment. A few nights ago she had been having a bit of mild flirtation on a girls' night out, but now the poor lass was quaking with fear in case I, or one of her friends, would let a word slip which might cause her husband to ask questions.

I felt for the girl, excused myself, and moved a safe distance away to ease the tension that gripped the poor lassie. Wearing the kilt had again proved beneficial - it provided a distraction for the husband and diverted his attention from asking awkward questions.

CHAPTER 15

Wonder-woman

A visit to Punanga Nui Market on a Saturday morning had become an almost obligatory activity. Shopping is far from being my favourite activity, but it was a good place for meeting people. I had no intention of buying anything other than some fruit, but wearing my kilt resulted in an unexpected purchase and the establishment of a cherished friendship that has lasted 20 years.

As I strolled past a colourful stall festooned with pareus for women and flamboyant shirts for men, the face of one of the girls working at the stall broke into a dazzling smile and she moved out to apprehend me.

"You are from Scotland!" she cried.

"Aye, how did you guess?"

"Your kilt, of course! I've been to Scotland. I love to see the men wearing their kilts." That shook me.

"What on earth was a Cook Island girl doing in Scotland?"

"I was performing in the Cook Islands dance team at the Edinburgh Festival at Edinburgh Castle. It was a fantastic experience."

"Ah, so you'll know Krystina Kauvai, the current Miss Tiare. I met her here last year and she told me she had danced there too."

"Oh, you know Krystina? Yes, there were lots of us in that team. It was an amazing experience to dance in front of 10,000 people on the castle esplanade."

I could well imagine. These girls and boys, in their teens, were performing at the Edinburgh International Festival of the Arts, the largest arts festival in the world. Only the best are invited to perform there and The Military Tattoo on the castle esplanade is the highlight, with military and civilian performers from all over the world presenting a spectacle that is a riot of colour and skill. I had seen that performance on TV. The Cook Islands dance team wowed the audience that year.

"It must have been chilly for you dancing in bare feet in a scanty Cook Islands costume in the Scottish weather!" I said.

"It was okay while we were dancing, but it was really cold while we were waiting in the castle courtyard before we went on." She chuckled. "But there were lots of young soldiers there offering to keep us warm. We stayed at the Queen Victoria School for Boys at Dunblane. It was a lot of fun. I'd love to go back to see more of Scotland some day. It's so beautiful there. Anyway, what are you doing here? It's a such long way from Scotland."

"I'm travelling around the world, but I'm staying here for several months to do some voluntary work in schools."

She then eyed me up and down. "The kilt looks great, but you really need a new shirt." She picked at my polo shirt. "Look at this old thing. It's almost worn through."

The shirt: super saleswoman, aged 14.

"It's still good for a few years," I protested, "there aren't any holes in it yet."

"But look at it! It's drab compared with your kilt. You need a nice new shirt to go with your kilt. Come over here and buy one." I couldn't resist as she dragged me over to the stall.

"I'm no good at this kind of thing. You'll need to pick one for me."

"Let's see." She gazed over the range of shirts and picked one. She held it against me. "Yes, try this one." She unbuttoned the shirt and slipped my arms into its sleeves. Then she buttoned me up and stood back a pace. "Yes, that looks much better."

I had my doubts. "Do you think so? Is it not too garish?"

"Of course not! It's perfect on you. It matches the blue colour of your eyes. You're in the South Pacific now. You need to brighten up your clothes and throw away that grubby old shirt."

I was overwhelmed. She was a charming girl: beautiful, smart, confident, and full of laughter. My resistance crumbled and I paid up. "Go in there and put your new shirt on now," she commanded, pointing to a changing area. She took my old shirt and put it in a plastic bag. "I'll throw this old thing in the bin."

My shirt did blend in with the colourful shirts worn by the local men. If it wasn't for the kilt, I could have been mistaken for just another Cook Island boy.

"Ko'ai to'ou ingoa?" I decided to practice my Cook Island Maori.

"Ah, you know how to speak Maori! Joyana Meyer," she replied, and shook me by the hand.

That was my introduction to another outstanding Cook Islands teenager with such confidence and maturity - she was still only 14 years old ! A couple of weeks later she succeeded Krystina as Miss Tiare. Both these talented girls went on to win the Miss Cook Islands and Miss South Pacific titles a few years further down the. line. Krystina studied Finance and Accounting in New Zealand and returned to Rarotonga to work for the government, married, and is now successful in the tourism business.

Winning the Miss Tiare title 2003, age 14

Miss South Pacific 2010

Graduate Mechatronics engineer

Joyana graduated in mechatronic engineering at the University of Auckland and has since designed and installed electronic-controlled engineering projects in different parts of the world. Now the mother of three young girls, she has written the first three in a series of children's science books to explain electrons, protons, and covalent chemical bonds to young children, using her own colourful designs and rhyming text to appeal to her young readership. These books are now being published in several countries.

Her artistic talent has also been applied to the design and production of fabrics embracing the vibrant colours of her native Rarotonga. She has appeared on New Zealand TV on numerous occasions and featured as a role model for girls in engineering, the living proof that women can succeed in science and engineering careers. Her achievements in such a variety of roles: dancer, beauty queen, graduate engineer, mother, wife, writer, speaker, book designer, fabric designer, female role model, surely entitle her to the additional appellation, 'Wonder-Woman.'

And when I gaze in wonder at the outrageously colourful shirt she persuaded me to buy, I would add outstanding saleswoman as well!

CHAPTER 16

Enigmatic Easter Island

Amazing, atmospheric, enigmatic: Easter Island is unique. Viewed from the air, its rather gaunt appearance was in stark contrast to the lush tropical growth to which I had become accustomed in the South Pacific. It reminded me of the Orkney Islands to the north of Scotland: grassy hills with hardly a tree to be seen, forbidding cliffs, and a rugged coastline where the ocean swells exploded white on black, saw-toothed rocks.

Its name in the local language is Rapa Nui, and most of its population of some 2000 people live in Hanga Roa, the island's only township. The rest is rolling grassland over ancient lava flows, grazed by free-roaming horses and a few cows, with extinct volcanoes at each end.

On the outer rim of the crater of Rano Raraku, an extinct volcano at the east end of the island, is the quarry where the famous Easter Island statues, the moai, were carved. These monster effigies were not cut from blocks of stone. They were painstakingly hewn out of an almost vertical rock face. The largest of them is twenty-two metres long (seventy feet) and its weight has been estimated at around 180 tonnes. Using only stone tools fashioned from hard basalt rock (metal was unknown here until the Europeans arrived), the islanders cut into the rock face and sculpted these enormous statues, somehow eased them out, and tipped them down the slope into pits to arrest their descent. From there they were transported across the island, some as far as 25 kilometres (over 15 miles).

Moai at quarry

Modern sculpture of stone chisel used

Various theories have been advanced to explain how this amazing feat might have been achieved. Legend tells us that they 'walked' across, and it has been demonstrated how this could have been done. One statue was walked back to the quarry from the other side of the island - at a speed of twenty-five kilometres per *month* - using 18 men with blocks and tackle and logs. The action was the same as you might use to ease a refrigerator out of a confined space in your kitchen, shuffling it a little to each side as you drag. Some argue that they may also have been laid flat on logs and rolled, and this method has also been demonstrated as possible, but raising the statues from the horizontal to the vertical position at the location presents a considerable challenge without a crane. Either way, it was a considerable feat of engineering.

Just about everything about Easter Island's history is intriguing. Only about 24 kilometres (15 miles) long by 16 kilometres (10 miles) at its widest, the fact that this tiny triangular island was ever discovered at all, and settled by the Polynesians, is remarkable. Even though they were great navigators and colonised most of the South Pacific islands, this is a tiny dot in the midst of an awful lot of ocean. To the south, the next landfall is Antarctica, about 5000 kilometres away. Mexico is about 8000 kilometres to the north. Chile, 3700 kilometres to the east, while Australia lies about 8000 kilometres to the west. Tahiti, French Polynesia, is a mere 4500 kilometres away. The Rapa Nui people didn't meet their neighbours very often.

Thor Heyerdal, the Norwegian explorer, argued that the first settlers may have come from the east. He demonstrated, with his Kon-Tiki Expedition in 1947, that it was possible to drift westwards on a balsa-wood raft from South America to Easter Island. However, in the absence of archaeological, linguistic, or cultural evidence to support this theory, it has been discredited. All the available evidence links the Rapa Nui people with Polynesian culture. The language is similar to Tahitian and Maori and the Polynesians are believed to have settled on the island around 400CE.

Deification of ancestors was an element of Polynesian culture, but the Rapa Nui people took it to extremes. They believed that honouring their ancestors by erecting the huge moai on their graves would bring the tribe great *mana* - a kind of spiritual power. Someone must have been persuasive. Imagine being told: "Right boys, let's take some small pieces of stone and hack away at that rock face until we have carved out a big statue. Then we'll drag it out and hoist it upright, and then - you'll enjoy this bit - we'll walk it...yes *walk* it...twenty-five kilometres to the other side of the island, and place it on top of the ahu, the stone platform that covers the graves of our ancestors. That will make us more powerful. And once we have it erected there, we can chisel out a big circular piece of rock to put on its head to resemble the way we wear our hair tied in a topknot. We'll work out another bit of clever engineering to hoist this big rock up, swing it over and centre it nicely on the head. Even better, if we do this several times and have... let's say... six of these monsters gazing at us, we'll be six times more powerful!"

Completed with eyes and topknot

Aye, right! Here was religious fervour gone mad.

And having convinced them that this was a worthwhile project, just think of the logistics: the management of teams of sculptors, woodcutters, road makers, and haulers; the logs, ropes, food supplies, and cooks. They had to be fed and watered while they worked. Modern sculptors reckon it would take twenty skilled men at least six months to create one statue. Trees had to be cut and transported to various locations for erection and rolling purposes, roadways prepared to make the transportation possible over the rough lava flows, and then there is the actual engineering involved in transportation. How did they work out how to do it? How did they know if they could even manage to move the first one? After that, they could apply their knowledge and experience. And as they learned more, they built more and bigger statues, until they reached that 22 metre, 180 tonne monster still lying at the quarry.

Around 800 statues exist of which about half have been moved to ceremonial sites where their chiefs were buried, mostly around the coast. They were erected with their backs to the sea to keep watch over the villages. The rest remain at the quarry.

Ceremonial site, keeping watch over the village

Most of the stone carving is thought to have taken place between the 6th and 17th century CE. By the time Captain Cook arrived in the late 18th century, most of the statues had been toppled. He described the people as poor, small, lean, timid, and miserable. In 1804, a Russian visitor recorded at least 20 moai still standing, but later disruption led to these all being pulled down. By the end of the 19th century, not one of the moai was left standing. So what happened to bring about such a dire change in attitude? Why were those in the quarry abandoned?

What happened here was a social catastrophe: a sudden, dramatic, and discontinuous change in social order brought about by an unsustainable lifestyle shaped by obsessive beliefs.

It is amazing that in spite of having developed such engineering and organisational skills, they seemed to have failed to realise the significance of cutting down every single tree on the island. Having denuded their habitat of trees, they had no more timber to build houses, light fires, or make canoes, without which they could neither escape the island, nor go to sea to fish offshore. The woodland habitat had been destroyed, and the wildlife with it. They had emptied the larder that fed them - and left themselves without the means of replenishing it.

Without the necessary logs to erect and move them, the remaining moai had to be abandoned at the quarry. The six tribes on the island who had competed with each other by building bigger moai were now confronted with starvation, and warred with each other over the island's diminishing resources. The next two centuries were characterised by the breakdown of social order on the island. Just as they had believed great power came from erecting the statues, they also reasoned that this power could be destroyed if the statues were pulled down, and they toppled each other's moai in their bid for supremacy. With starvation an ever-present threat, they resorted to cannibalism - they hadn't left themselves much choice. The population prior to the period of social disintegration has been estimated at around 15,000 people. Within two hundred years it had plummeted to about 2000. But that wasn't the end of their misery.

In 1862, a raid by slave traders from Peru transported a thousand islanders to the Chincha Islands, to work the guano deposits there. Nine hundred of them perished, but after intense pressure from the Catholic Church, the survivors were shipped back home. However, this humane act by the church had tragic consequences. Some of those released had contracted smallpox, and by the time the ship arrived at Easter Island, only fifteen were still alive. They took the disease ashore with them, and the island's population was decimated once more. It is claimed that only 111 people survived the smallpox epidemic.

Easter Island is a thought-provoking place. It could well be a metaphor for planet Earth. We may marvel that the people who lived here had been blind to the damage they were doing to their environment and could not foresee the social consequences. Their engineering achievements were remarkable, but their leaders carried too much authority and the people mindlessly followed the doctrine - until it was too late.

But wait a minute, let's not be too smug. Look at our own history. A quick glance at the history of the twentieth century and the early years of the twenty-first, let alone all that happened before, shows that we have no right to feel superior. We have endured two world wars and numerous other conflicts, global exploitation of human and natural resources, and the spoliation of the environment in the pursuit of commercial gain, with excessive power, political and economic, concentrated in the hands of a tiny minority. But are they safe hands? Are we, too, being led along a route to self-destruction? The example of Easter Island could be a valuable element in the education of us all.

Though it came perilously close to extinction, the population of Easter Island survived - just - and is becoming prosperous once more. The extension of the airfield runway (as a possible emergency landing site for the US space shuttle) gave the island a viable international airport and tourism has grown. Large cruise ships visit the island from time to time, but the long sea-crossing to get there remains a limiting factor in the number of ships that will call. It is still a relatively unspoilt island and, given its remote location, is likely to remain so. However, its accessibility by air offers its inhabitants the opportunity to enjoy a more secure future based on tourism - if they are careful and conserve what they have. Had their ancestors not left them something unique, the moai, few would ever come to such a remote place. Ironically, the obsession with the creation of the moai that led to almost complete desolation, is bringing prosperity to the island's people at last. You get the feeling that this place deserves some good fortune.

The population is now a mix of Polynesian and Chilean, with a sprinkling of European blood as well. Having been annexed by Chile in the late 19th century, the official language is Spanish, but Rapa Nui is still their native language and Polynesian influences are dominant in music, dance, and art.

The tourist guide-books may tell you three days is enough to see everything, but it was not enough for me. I arrived on a Monday morning from Tahiti and left on Thursday afternoon for Santiago, but that was too rushed. I would have preferred more time to do some walking and for photography, taking advantage of the early morning and evening light. I never even had time to visit the museum, or savour the social life of the community.

Monday to Thursday is the quiet period, with nothing happening in the evenings. I was told that the weekend is the time to be here, when the place is jumping, with music and dancing all night long, but I couldn't delay my flight out as I had connections to make in South America.

"That's a pity," said one of the local ladies. She flicked her eyebrows, "With that kilt you could get up to some mischief here!"

CHAPTER 17

Theft

T he flight from Easter Island to Santiago proved very
pleasant, thanks to the English girl seated next to me:
"Wow! I didn't expect to see a Scottish kilt on Easter Island! What
are you doing here?" We talked throughout the entire journey,
during which she learned that I hadn't a word of Spanish in me.
She worked for a Spanish printing company in Madrid and had
been posted to Chile to look after the company's interests there.
Like me, she had taken a short break to see Rapa Nui and, as we
belted up for landing at Santiago, she told me, "Now, you do realise
that you are coming in my taxi and I'll drop you off at your hostel."

How could I resist such an assertive woman? I mumbled my
thanks and within twenty minutes of leaving the airport I was
checking into my hostel for an overnight stop.

The morning was bright and sunny; a good day to fly over the
Andes. Every mountain, valley, river could be seen with clarity, but
what surprised me was how narrow the Andes range of mountains
is: we were over it in a few minutes. The remainder of the flight
was over flat country: the grassland that produces the famed
Argentinian beef that owes its quality to the fine breeding bulls
imported from Scotland. Again, I had a good travel companion.
The Argentinian in the seat next to me spoke very good English
and offered to help me by writing out some useful words and

phrases. He said he would meet me in the arrivals hall after I had cleared immigration and would help me find a taxi to take me to my hostel. He was being met by his girlfriend, but was heading in the opposite direction; otherwise, he would have given me a lift.

Having cleared immigration, I looked around the arrivals hall for my Argentinian friend. A middle-aged man approached. "Excuse me sir, you are from Scotland? I hope you don't mind if I introduce myself. My name is Duncan MacKinlay. One of my ancestors was from Scotland. It is so nice to see you wearing your national dress and I wondered if there is anything I can do to help you. Do you speak Spanish?"

"Not a word. Thanks for the offer, but I'm looking for a friend, an Argentinian I met on the plane, who said he would help me find a taxi."

"Oh well, in that case I'll leave you my business card, and if there is ever any need for help, with interpreting or whatever, please do not hesitate to contact me. How long are you staying in Buenos Aires?"

"Only one night."

"Oh, what a pity. I would have liked to invite you to my home to meet the rest of my family. We are very proud of our Scottish ancestry."

At that point, the guy from the plane arrived. I explained who my new friend was and introduced them. He laughed, "Now I can understand why you wear your kilt," he said, "it is a good way to meet people."

My kilt attracted more than a few glances when I dined out that night. An American couple were seated at a neighbouring table. When my steak and chips arrived, I heard the man say to his wife, "Those French fries look real good."

"Go on, have some. There are more on the plate than I can manage."

Initially embarrassed, he was soon tempted to lay his inhibitions aside in the knowledge that he would be doing me a favour by taking some. A few minutes later, a glass of beer arrived at my table. The waiter indicated with a brief flourish that this came with the compliments of my American friend. I looked over and acknowledged his hospitality.

"That's very kind of you. Thank you very much."

"Well, you were kind enough to give me some of your fries."

I laughed. "Aye, but I think I got the better part of the deal." When they had eaten and were starting their coffee they invited me to join them. Both ornithologists, they taught in Boston and had visited Scotland a few years previously to study the bird life in the Shetland Isles. They were now on their way home from Antarctica.

Buenos Aires was proving to be more pleasant than I had anticipated. On my way back to the hostel, I met two young men who wanted to have photographs taken with me. They were football fans and knew more about the current state of Scottish football than I did. They have it all on TV there. I was beginning to like Buenos Aires. Its people were proving to be so friendly that I regretted having scheduled only one night there.

After breakfast and a shower, I packed my bags and called a taxi. I was at the airport more than two hours before my flight to Ushuaia was due, but I thought I could check-in my luggage, then have something to eat. I took my passport, return flight ticket for Ushuaia, and my wallet out of my hand luggage and stuck them in my sporran, ready for use at the cafe and check-in desk. I was turned away: check-in for internal flights starts one hour before the time of the flight. I found a seat at the end of a row and laid my rucksack on the floor in front of me and my hand luggage down by my right leg. I wasn't ready to eat just yet.

For the first time ever, wearing the kilt brought misfortune. An Englishman, currently living in Aberdeen, spotted it and sat beside me. He had just arrived from Scotland, having been delayed by hurricane force winds a few days previously. I had heard about this in an email from home. We chatted for about twenty minutes. I had half-turned towards him as we talked, and when I turned back, the hand luggage that had been sitting on the floor by my right leg had disappeared. In it was my laptop computer, my expensive new digital camera and all the photos taken in the four months I had been travelling, cellphone, travellers cheques, plane tickets... All gone! The initial sickening feeling was counter-balanced by the relief that I had my wallet with some cash and credit card, my passport, and the ticket for the return flight to Ushuaia in my sporran ready for the check-in.

But my good feelings about Buenos Aires had evaporated.

I had to file a report with the airport police and just managed it in time to catch my flight to Ushuaia. The police had telephoned the check-in desk and made special arrangements for me, and an officer escorted me through. He shook hands with me and said, "I would like to apologise on behalf of my country for this despicable incident. I hope you will find that most Argentinians are very hospitable people who are happy to welcome you to our country."

I had plenty of time to reflect on my folly during the four-hour flight south to Ushuaia on Tierra del Fuego, the island at the southern end of South America. However, I resolved not to let that bit of misfortune spoil what had been such a memorable trip up to that point. Weighing it all up, I had some great memories. I was still alive and well; I had my passport, cash, and credit card. I would get some financial recompense from the travel insurance and I could replace the computer, camera, and phone. I could arrange for new plane tickets to be issued. And I resolved to return some day to Easter Island to replace the photographs that had been stolen. Ahead of me lay a trek in the spectacular mountains of Patagonia and what could possibly be the most memorable experience of all - a trip to Antarctica. My accommodation in Ushuaia was very good and dinner that night was excellent. There was no point in being miserable. Everything would get sorted out - eventually.

A major telecommunications fault had developed somewhere between Tierra del Fuego and the rest of the world. Telephone contact was impossible: not even mobile phones would work, and all the computer links were down. The shops could not use their credit card links, and the banks had to close. The airlines could not access their booking systems, so I couldn't get my flight tickets re-issued. I couldn't email and I couldn't telephone to contact my insurers, or anyone else. I reverted to old-fashioned letter writing, but the post office was choked with people who had been forced to do the same, and I had to wait in a queue for 45 minutes to buy a stamp. Business in Ushuaia went into meltdown. Well, that's a dramatic way of saying they shrugged and decided there was no point in hanging around, so they all had a holiday. *Que sera, sera.* I shrugged and had a day off too.

I surprised myself at the way I had accepted the situation, refusing to let it get me down. Could I have handled this as well before I started travelling? Then, even the slightest mishap had a tendency to be blown out of proportion in a mind that demanded perfection. The ability to adapt to unforeseen circumstances is essential on extended, independent travel. Next day, when the fault had been repaired, it was business as usual. I managed to make the necessary arrangements and replaced my camera, finding the same model in Ushuaia. I could not go to Antarctica without a camera.

Ushuaia has an Alpine feel to it. The most southern city in the world, it is very much a frontier town, with Cape Horn just around the corner. To the south, beyond Cape Horn, lie the most turbulent seas in the world, and Antarctica, the emptiest place in the world. To the North, there was also a lot of emptiness with very little habitation in the 2000 miles between Ushuaia and Buenos Aires. The Patagonian plain is a cool desert. Dirt roads crossed this arid plain, but seldom was there a vehicle to be seen on them. On Tierra del Fuego, the island changes from desert plain to jagged mountains.

And there, on the edge of the Beagle Channel, lies Ushuaia, 'the city at the end of the world'.

CHAPTER 18

Patagonia

E l Calafate, an hour's flying time north from Ushuaia, is a small town on the edge of a national park famed for its mountains and glaciers. My Patagonian trek had been booked with a company called GAP Adventures, the Great Adventure People. There were five of us in the group. Natasha, our courier, shepherded us to the airport at Ushuaia and had a minibus organised to pick us up at El Calafate. Half English-half Peruvian, she spoke fluent Spanish.

Driving towards El Calafate from the airport, the landscape looked like a scene from a Hollywood western; an arid, ochre terrain dotted by desert scrub with an inhospitable chill wind blowing over it.

"There's always a wind in Patagonia," said Natasha, "so be prepared. Even if the day starts still and warm, a wind will blow up from somewhere."

And dust. Road vehicles traversed this terrain like comets, a long tail of dust marking their transit across the desert.

To the east, the rolling plain stretched up to a plateau, the Patagonian steppeland, and to the west the mountains were darkening in the light of the setting sun. I had never been attracted to deserts, but this place had an alluring, atmospheric quality about it in the soft, golden light of the setting sun. It would be a good place to explore with a camera. In the morning, as we headed west into the mountains, our local mountain guide told us how this landscape and been created.

The Andes Mountains were thrust up from the Pacific Ocean around 65 million years ago, and they are still rising about one centimetre per year. Some parts are as young as only 12 million years, geological infants compared with the gnarled, old crags formed between 1000 million and 4000 million years ago where I live in the northwest highlands of Scotland.

The prevailing wind is westerly. It sweeps in from the Pacific Ocean laden with moisture, and the air is forced to rise when it encounters the massive wall of rock that is the Andes. As the air chills, the moisture condenses and precipitates as rain on the west side, snow on the mountain tops, and by the time it has crossed the icy summits, the moisture has been extracted, so there is nothing left to drop on the east side except cool air, hence the cold desert plain of Santa Cruz that stretches all the way to the Atlantic coast.

Covering the high ground is the Patagonian ice-cap, the third largest source of fresh water in the world behind the two polar regions, where compressed snow forms an enormous ice-field from which numerous large glaciers grind their way downwards, ending in pale turquoise-coloured lakes. The characteristic colour is caused by minute mineral particles ground from the rocks by the glacier and held in suspension in the water. This ice-cap is the source of the infamous Patagonian wind. As the air in the valleys warms it becomes less dense and rises, allowing the dense cold air above the ice-cap to come roaring down the mountains, sometimes with astounding ferocity.

Our destination that day was the Perito Morena Glacier. A trek round the lake took us to its terminal wall of ice, 60 metres high and over 2000 metres wide. Probably the fastest moving glacier in the world, it slides forward at an average rate of 1.7 metres per day, shedding lumps of ice with a crack like thunder, huge blocks crashing into the lake every few minutes. This spot is accessible by road, and busloads of tourists arrive daily to view the ice show and have their pictures taken by professional photographers, with the glacier in the background,

Perito Morena Glacier

But the glacier had a competitor that day. Having done the trek in my kilt, I was getting as many people wanting to pose with me as the professional photographers were with their glacier. Hordes of Argentinian women snuggled up to me, put their arms around my waist, and ordered their husbands to operate the cameras. One of the ladies engaged me in conversation about the kilt and Scotland and told me her surname was MacKinlay.

"You are the second person I have met with that name since arriving in Argentina," I said. "I met a man called Duncan MacKinlay at the airport in Buenos Aires."

"Oh, you have met Duncan? He is my cousin," she said.

Later that evening, as I waited to board a bus at El Calafate, another lady approached me. "I am so pleased to see you wearing your kilt," she said. "I have Scottish ancestors. My name is Guadaloupe MacKinlay."

She was as amazed as I was that I had met her uncle Duncan and her aunt already. These three MacKinlays were descendants of a 19th century farmer from the Isle of Bute, not far from where I was born, who was one of the pioneers of the beef trade in Argentina, arriving there in 1804. Argentina is a huge country with a disproportionately small population of only around 37 million, yet I had met three relatives descended from the same Scottish farmer, 2000 miles apart, within my first few days. The probability of that happening is so small it made me think it might be worth buying a ticket in the national lottery.

A five-hour bus ride over the bumpy dirt roads of the desert took us to a wee place called El Chalten. It consists of a scattering of small, lapboard shacks, one or two modest hotels, a couple of shops bearing the ubiquitous red coca-cola sign, dirt roads, no sidewalks, and a mournful wind that sweeps through its only street, whipping up small tornadoes of dust. This looked like spaghetti western country and I wouldn't have been surprised to meet Clint Eastwood and Lee van Cleef in a shoot out. Until recently there was no town, only a sheep station. El Chalten owes its existence to the trekkers and mountaineers who come to explore the nearby wonderland of spectacular mountains and glaciers.

In the morning, a long trek through forests of southern beech led us to a glacial valley and over a heap of terminal moraine, marking where the glacier had reached 150 years ago - it had now retreated about a kilometre back from that position. Before us lay a fairy-tale scene. Beyond a small glacial lake rose Los Torres, a scenic wonderland of elegant rock spires: silvery-grey pinnacles of granite with sheer walls that soared skywards, their feet swathed in winding, deep-furrowed glaciers. We sat on the shore of the lake eating our packed lunches and marvelled at the splendour before us. It was the most surreal landscape I had ever encountered.

However, the nine-hour trek the following day to Mount Fitzroy surpassed even that. One of the most dramatic mountains in the world, it was named in honour of Captain Fitzroy of HMS Beagle, the survey ship that took Charles Darwin on his famous voyage of discovery to the Galapagos Islands. The ship's boats had explored this area, rowing 200 km up the Santa Cruz River. The last pitch was a scramble up 350 metres (about 1150 feet) of moraine, requiring the use of hands as well as feet. It was energy sapping work, but the view at the top was spectacular.

Mount Fitzroy, like an elongated nipple with sheer faces, soared 3400 metres (over 11000 feet) into an azure sky. Its attendant glacier, like a scarf wrapped around its shoulders, curved down to melt into a turquoise lake. Through the binoculars I could see two tiny figures clinging high on one of the rock faces, painstakingly making their way towards the peak. That put the magnitude of the mountain into perspective. Our guide told us he had climbed Mt Fitzroy. It had taken five days, and at night they had to bivouac on the precipitous slopes, lashed on to slim ledges in biting cold winds. Technically it is a difficult climb, but the fickle weather is the real enemy of the mountaineer. Exposure takes on a new meaning on these icy, wind-scoured slabs.

Mount Fitzroy

The climb up the moraine had been tough, but the way down was painful. With so much loose rock and scree it was potentially dangerous, and my knees, taking the strain, suffered burning pain. I regretted leaving my trekking poles behind that day, a mistake I would not repeat. A pleasant diversion on the way back was a detour to cool off in a picturesque lake before attempting the final descent down to El Chalten. The trek had been challenging and the body knew it had done some work, but after a hot shower it glowed. Sleep came easily that night.

At Mount Fitzroy

Reveille was at 6:00 a.m. to catch the bus that would take us to Chile. At the border, we disembarked to have our bags checked by a team of customs officers. While I waited in the queue, a female officer called out to me, "Hey, come over here." I lifted my baggage on to the bench for inspection, but she said, "Never mind your baggage. Let's see your kilt." After a few moments discussion about it, she passed me through without examining my bags.

Chile matched Argentina in both the beauty and power of its landscape. The treks were strenuous but rewarding, with unforgettable scenery. In the Asciena Valley, a skyline of towering crags gave way to long scree slopes sprinkled with a few patches of tenacious vegetation. The scree tumbled into the V-shaped valley where a gushing white river cascaded over rocks far below. The trek took us along a narrow path, with hundreds of feet of scree slopes down to the river, or along rock faces bordering the river. Another scramble, 370 metres (1200 feet) up an enormous heap of glacial debris had to be scaled to secure the ultimate reward for our labours. Towering above the far side of another glacial lake, a series of granite peaks, the Torres del Paine, pointed their fingers into the sky for another 2000 metres or more (7000 feet). These soaring pinnacles, a magnet for climbers, test the skills of the best mountaineers in the world.

Torres del Paine

They are also a magnet for photographers, and charmed us that day with a striptease show. Drawing swirling clouds around their peaks, they shrouded themselves in mystery, offering only an occasional, ghostly glimpse. A few moments later, the warmth of the sun drew breezes that cast aside the white drapes and they exposed themselves once more, revealing the glory of their rugged beauty against a backcloth of blue sky. Their feet lay swathed in the icy wraps of curling glaciers that died on a sun-kissed shelf of rock. There, the ice melted into hundreds of streams of water, painting the rock face with dark stripes where the melt-water flowed over the rock into the lake.

This was a place to rest; restoring tired bodies with food, filling cameras with images, gazing in wonder at a landscape changing in tone and texture as clouds danced and swirled around its peaks. It was difficult to drag ourselves away, such was the power of this ever-changing scene. It would have been interesting to spend the night up there in order to capture the glowing colours of the rocks reflecting the red light of dawn, but our tents were already pitched at a campsite four hours walking time away, so we had to prise ourselves out of this rocky paradise and descend once more.

Campsites are sociable places, and sitting around the campfire late at night telling stories can be one of their great pleasures. Herñan, our mountain guide, was a likeable wee Chilean who had married an English girl. He sat opposite me, wide-eyed as I recited the poem Tam O' Shanter (an epic tale of witches and warlocks), with the light and shadow of the flickering flames dancing on my face. Before going to bed he told me, "John, I wish I'd had a video camera with me. That's the kind of storytelling I'd love my children to hear."

It was low-level walks the following day, in lashing rain and a howling wind in the morning, catching glimpses of Los Quernos (The Horns), another set of spectacular mountain peaks. A boat trip in the afternoon took us up the Grey Lake to view the glacier at its northern end. The Grey Glacier is quite stable, so the boat could get relatively close to its towering walls, fissured with crevasses, and sculpted into pinnacles of pale blue ice. We disembarked at a campsite below the glacier, with a cool wind sweeping down from the ice-fields. The wind was welcome though. Hanging up our sodden clothing at the campsite, the blustery wind had it dried before bedtime.

Los Quernos

Having arrived the easy way, by boat, we walked out through the mountains. That last trek was a joy. The rain stayed away, the fresh wind on our backs prevented us from becoming too hot, and the sun shone through the broken clouds scudding across the mountains. The week's trekking had hardened the feet, and the knees were no longer complaining. Lungs had been cleansed, the blood purified by clean mountain air. Muscles were well-toned, and it was a joy to go pounding up and down the slopes, feeling the body working like a well-oiled machine. Such a sense of well- being and general fitness was euphoric. My youth had been restored, and it was with considerable sadness that I viewed the end of our meandering trek through the mountains of Patagonia. A ferry transported us across the lake to where a minibus waited to take us to Puerto Natales.

Herñan, our guide, was one of those special people with whom I had felt an instant connection. We'd talked a lot during our treks and sitting beside him in the minibus on the way back, we both fell asleep. Our heads rolled sideways and our bodies collapsed against each other. His head rested on my shoulder, tucked under my cheek; my head leaned on top of his, using it as a pillow. Amused by the sight of two tired amigos snoring in affectionate harmony, someone took a camera out to capture the moment.

At Puerto Natales, when we said our goodbyes, Herñan hugged me. "John, my amigo," he told me, "I wanna come to Scotland to hear more of your stories. That night at the camp fire was the highlight of the trip for me."

CHAPTER 19

Drake Passage

"How many of you have brought seasickness pills?" Ian Shaw, the expedition leader, started our initial briefing on board the ship, Explorer, bound for the Antarctic peninsula. A forest of hands went up. "I see few of you haven't…"

I was one of those who didn't raise a hand. I was an experienced sailor in the often turbulent seas around Scotland. The pause, and the way he tucked his chin into his chest and looked over his non-existent spectacles, expressed his silent disapproval - the typical schoolmaster pose - I'd used it often enough. "Let me tell you about the Drake Passage…" He used the pause again to good effect.

"You are about to enter the most turbulent and unpredictable sea in the world, a place where even the most experienced mariners throw up. The wind here travels all the way round the world, unhindered by any land, except when it is funnelled between Cape Horn and the Graham Land peninsula on Antarctica. Because of this long fetch by the wind, the seas build up to enormous heights: waves 50 metres high (166 feet) are not uncommon. Ocean currents, deflected by the land masses of South America and Antarctica, interfere with the main stream running through from west to east to produce even more violent and very steep seas. The most experienced sailors take anti-seasickness medication here, so if you haven't brought any, my advice is to buy some now at the ship's reception desk. And don't make the mistake of waiting to see if you are going to feel sick first and then take the pills. It will be too late then. Seasickness pills are preventative, not curative, and should be taken before you start the voyage. The only way to cure seasickness is to go and sit under a tree..."

He paused for a moment to let the futility of that sink in. Silence. I admired his technique. He used these pauses good effect. We were now steaming down the sheltered waters of the Beagle Channel between Tierra Del Fuego and the group of islands to the south, which constitute the tail of the South American continent, culminating in Cape Horn.

"And let me tell you something else. Seasickness is ten times worse on an empty stomach, so eat plenty. We provide food all through the day for that very reason."

He'd told a good story, so I decided to play safe and get some pills. After all, this was supposed to be a trip undertaken for pleasure. Even if the sea is rough it can still be enjoyable, but not if you are bombarding other passengers with the contents of your stomach. It's a personal thing, but I don't like to share my vomit with anyone else. Whether it was the pills, or my experience as a sailor, I don't know, but I had no problem. Many others were sick in spite of taking the medication.

Explorer was designed and built in Finland in 1969 for polar exploration. A tough wee vessel with a double-strengthened hull, she carried a maximum of 108 passengers, and around 50 of a crew. She was reputed to be the ship that would boldly go where no other ship could in these waters. She had been the first ship to carry passengers to the Antarctic; the first passenger ship to navigate south of the Antarctic Circle; the first ship to take passengers through the North West Passage between Canada and the Arctic ice cap; and on her way from one end of the world to the other, she cruised 2000 miles up the Amazon, as far as Iquitos in Peru. Having had a major refit a few months earlier, she was now ready to push the limits once more. Her small size, reinforced hull, and shallow draught allowed us to force our way into narrow, ice-filled channels to reach some interesting landing spots. Her crew, many of whom had sailed in her for several years, regarded her with great affection - always a good sign. By the end of the voyage, most of the passengers felt the same way. She had a winning way with her.

Explorer

Despite her strengthened hull, in November 2007 she struck ice and sank. All the passengers and crew were rescued.

The briefing went on to describe what we could do, weather permitting, where we would try to go, the safety procedures, and the domestic arrangements. The captain introduced the officers, all Europeans, but the rest of the crew were Filipino, with four

Filipinas (females) to clean the cabins and serve as waitresses. It was a pleasure to meet such cheerful people as they went about their work each day. Melody, the girl who cleaned my room and served in the dining room, never failed to greet me with a smile and a cheery, "Good morning, sir."

"Och, call me John." I suggested.

Next day I was greeted with, "Good morning, Sir John." I had the honour of being the only person during the voyage to be elevated to a knighthood.

The other members of the expedition team introduced themselves. Experts on birds, marine mammals, Antarctic history, geography, geology, and photography educated us with lectures on our way southwards, and helped us interpret what we saw when we got there.

I looked around the assembled passengers. Most were aged between 30 and 60, with some teenagers in a couple of families from the USA, and several students in their early twenties. Antarctica is one of the most extreme environments on Earth. Being over 60, I had to have a medical certificate to testify that I was fit to undertake such an expedition.

Looking round the faces and observing the body language, I could sense an affiliation with some already. My gut feeling once more proved correct. During the trip, though we mixed randomly most of the time, social groupings tended to form and I found myself drawn to a group which consisted of those in their twenties or early thirties. They were the people most likely to gather round me at the dinner table. When the boats were being loaded with people to go ashore, I was corralled into this group with cries of "C'mon John, you're coming with us!" When I remarked on the thirty to forty year age gap between me and the rest of this young group I was told, "Ah, but this is not the young group. It is the young-at-heart-group, so you qualify."

The weather was kind to us on the way south with no more than a moderate breeze and a rolling swell. Sleep came easily in such conditions. But so did regurgitated food. On my way to the dining room next morning someone's breakfast had already made a hasty exit and was being cleaned off the carpet by a smiling Filipino steward. The next two days passed with a series of interesting lectures, interspersed with opportunities to photograph the mastery of flight of the albatrosses following the ship.

Swooping low behind our stern, with motionless wings they glided swiftly alongside, soared upwards, flipped over and circled round behind us once more in an aerial ballet performed with effortless grace. It is difficult to judge just how big these beautiful birds are in such a spacious environment, but the largest of the species, the wandering albatross, has a wingspan of more than three metres (ten feet). Capturing their flight on camera presented some challenges, but the digital camera proved its worth here. So many images could be shot and you could edit and get at least a few that were worth keeping. Having witnessed such advantages, several people were converted to digital photography during the trip, and the ship did a good trade in hiring out digital cameras.

During the voyage, people got to know one another. We had a group of twenty- seven Portuguese on board, three of whom were journalists: one from a magazine, one from radio, and one from a TV company, with a camera crew. Wearing my kilt at dinner on the first night, I got to know them all. They invited me over to their tables for introductions, photographs, and the usual admiring looks from the Portuguese ladies. Enthusiastic and determined to enjoy every experience the voyage had to offer, they were always the last to go to bed. They were easy to identify as they all wore red jackets emblazoned with Expedition To The End Of The World on their backs.

It was one of the Portuguese who was first to spot an iceberg on the evening of the second day. Dinner that night was punctuated by cries of delight as another iceberg was spotted and the ship listed to one side as people left their tables to rush over to see the latest lump of ice. Twenty-four hours later icebergs had become such a familiar part of the scene they were seldom mentioned.

First sight of Antacrtica

That night, as the ship laboured through the grinding ice flows in the Gerlache Strait, most people were on deck taking pictures. Mountains clothed in deep snow rose from the sea on both sides of the channel; whales lay motionless on the surface, and seals languished on ice flows. It was a windless night with the ice tinted by the warm glow of the sunset at around 11p.m. Even after the sun had slipped behind the mountains, the afterglow continued throughout the night and everyone seemed reluctant to go to bed.

We had been told in the briefing that a visit to Antarctica could prove to be a life-changing experience. Many people who have come to this most forbidding of continents find it addictive, compelling them to return. In this land of extremes nothing inhabits the realm of ordinariness. It is the coldest, windiest, and driest place on earth. It is the world's largest desert and has, surprisingly, an average of less than 2 inches of snowfall per year over the entire continent. Deep in the interior it may not snow for years at a time, but the wind blows it about. Its sheer isolation can induce 'Polar madness,' a condition first identified by a scientist who travelled with Scott and Shackleton.

This condition can have serious consequences. During a game of chess some years back, a Soviet scientist was killed by his opponent wielding an ice-axe. The Soviet authorities responded by banning the game of chess! An American expedition led by Admiral Byrd, the first man to fly over the South Pole, recognised the risks and had two coffins and twelve straight-jackets listed in its inventory. I looked around the faces in the lecture room, wondering...strange things could happen in a place like this.

Despite its forbidding nature, it has an alluring beauty and sense of peace. Five weeks after our return, Geraldine, a 23 year-old French girl, wrote to me:

> 'I have never felt better in my life than when I was there. It's difficult to explain. The best description I can use is that it was a spiritual experience. It's an ideal setting to think about the meaning of life and all those related philosophical thoughts. There was no daily hassle, no time. Day and night

were meaningless as it never got dark. It was all stress-free, experiencing and feeling life in a new light. You just let yourself get absorbed by nature. Hearing, or seeing, glaciers break apart, watching penguins swimming, feeding, running after one another, making sounds to recognise their mates, swapping space over the nest to keep their eggs warm. Watching leopard seals relax on icebergs; smelling the fishy odour of the whales' breath. Looking out from the bridge windows on the ship, taking millions of photos. These memories have left deep marks on me'

My first image of Antarctica was gained as a boy, when I was one of thousands of British schoolchildren to troop through the doors of their local cinemas to watch the film, *Scott of the Antarctic*. Made in 1948, starring John Mills, it was considered to be of educational value and a special showing was arranged for schoolchildren. The heroic - though some argued stupid and ill-prepared - attempt by Captain Robert Falcon Scott to be first to reach the South Pole had captured the imagination of the British establishment. Here was a hero who gallantly died in the attempt, a glorious failure in the best traditions of the British Empire. The visual images of that film stuck in my mind: the icebergs, the striking contrast between the blue of the sea and the white of the snowfields and glaciers, the terrifying crevasses, the flimsy tents flapping in the ferocious, howling wind that tormented Scott's party on the return from the Pole, and the blizzards that prevented them from reaching the food at a supply depot only eleven miles away.

I had harboured a desire to see this for myself, but always it seemed so remote, so unreachable. It could never be more than a dream - but my dream was now being realised.

CHAPTER 20

Revealing Secrets

We had hoped to make it as far south as the Ukranian Vernadsky Base, a former British research station called Faraday, which had been handed over to the Ukranians. It had a unique claim to fame - it had the only pub in Antarctica!

Back in the 1950s, two British carpenters had been hired to construct a hardwood extension to the pier, but with the weather conditions preventing any outside work being done they passed the time building a classic English pub instead. The wharf was never completed and the men were dismissed. However, their immortality has been assured in the magnificent polished woodwork of the bar, a facility now treasured by the Ukranians. I was looking forward to wandering into the most southerly pub in the world wearing my kilt, but although the ship could force its way through, the ice floes proved too much for the zodiacs, the rigid inflatable boats we used for landings, so we couldn't get ashore.

Instead, Explorer thrust her way though to Petermann Island, home to a colony of Adelie penguins and some blue eyed shags. We dropped anchor close to the site of a British research camp, the first of several we encountered along the peninsula. It comprised a wooden hut and a scattering of yellow tents secured somehow to a few patches of unyielding granite rock. The scientists there were monitoring the impact of human interaction with the penguins.

Adele Penguin   Gentoo Penguin   Chindtrap Penguin

Despite its barren appearance and inhospitable reputation, Antarctica is a bustling global laboratory and museum. For here, written in the rocks and ice, is much of the story of the planet Earth: the origins of its life, the movement of continents, the ever-changing climate are all archived in its rock and ice strata. That so much life can survive here in such extreme conditions is astonishing. Tiny microscopic mites living under frost-shattered rocks have developed their own antifreeze, a glycerol type of compound. Giant humpback whales daily filter and digest tons of krill, the small shrimp-like crustacean which is at the core of the food chain here.

It was the ancient Greeks who theorised that, in order to maintain the balance of a spherical world, the land mass of the northern hemisphere must be counterbalanced by a significant mass of land somewhere in the south. Described in Latin on early maps as *Terra Australis Nondum Cognita* (the southern land as yet unknown), it remained so until its discovery in the early 19th century. Captain Cook had been sent to try to find this continent - if indeed it was a continent, for it could have been just a collection of islands - and was the first navigator known to have crossed the Antarctic Circle.

His first attempt was blocked by pack ice, but he retreated to Polynesia and returned the following summer, reaching 71 degrees south, a good ten degrees further than anyone had ever gone before. But Cook had gone to the wrong places, probing deep into the continent's broad bays. Blocked again by ice, he wrote in his journal: *"Ambition leads me not only further than any other man has been before me, but as far as I think it possible for man to go."* Had he explored just a bit to the east, he would have come to the Graham Land Peninsula, the long arm of land reaching up towards South America, where we were now.

Time proved him wrong and the continental land mass was discovered in the early 19th century. A gradual interest in Antarctica developed until the 1890s when a mixture of imperial ambition, scientific curiosity, and a thirst for good adventure stories by the media inspired an eruption of enthusiasm for polar exploration, culminating in the rush to be first to reach both the North and South Poles in the early 20th century. While the expeditions of Scott and Shackleton (both good publicists) are renowned, other expeditions have proved to be much more valuable from a scientific point of view. Today the research goes on by scientists from all over the world. Camping in tiny yellow tents while doing fieldwork, or analysing data in laboratories in heated buildings at the major bases, their research is revealing much of the natural history of this planet.

Evidence from rock samples has proved that these frozen wastes once supported tropical forests. This suggests, not that there has been a dramatic change in climate, but that this continent was once located much further north as part of a landmass in the tropics. As the world's continents have drifted apart, it has been the fate of this particular continent to drift southwards to endure the frozen eternity that is Antarctica.

Studies of glacial activity show how ice sheets can alter the climate of the planet. Global warming is an issue of major concern. Research on glacier margins and ice cores reveals evidence that the Earth's climate is far from stable. The short period of time over which meteorological records have been kept is minuscule on the scale of the earth's climate history, so that the warming we have now may be a minor blip, which could be followed by a rapid descent into another cold period. No one knows for sure, and the research continues. The issue is a complex one: 18,500 years ago when Scotland lay under a covering of ice around 5000 feet deep, South Georgia was de-glaciating. In the so-called Mini Ice Age between 1500 and 1900, many glaciers advanced beyond their normal limits. Recession from those limits represented the end of that cold period. The present warming may to some extent be a natural phenomenon, but the *rate of change* in average global temperature in the past few decades is a powerful indicator that it may be due to mankind's activities, particularly our pollution of the atmosphere by carbon emissions. Whatever the truth may be, Antarctica has much of the planet's history locked away in the fastness of its ice.

Antarctica is more accessible than ever before. Polar tourism has expanded in the last few decades, and at the time of writing (2010), around 25,000 visitors were arriving each year. But don't expect to see an Antarctic Hilton Hotel standing on these ice-girt shores. On our way south, I heard one passenger from the USA ask, "What are the restaurants like in Antarctica? What kind of food do they eat there?" Despite the information on the internet and documentaries available on television, some people imagine it is inhabited by tribes of southern Inuits, living in igloos, hunting polar bears, but there are none of them either - they are confined to the northern polar regions. There are no land-based mammals in Antarctica; only marine mammals such as seals, sea lions, and whales. There are no towns. The only inhabitants are a few temporary residents in the scientific bases. It is the emptiest place on earth.

In this sensitive environment, all tour operators must subscribe to a strict code of practice. Prior to every excursion ashore, we were briefed on environmental issues. Foot-baths were set out for us on the ship to minimise the risk of carrying infection from one site to another. Nothing must be left behind. Body waste management was therefore important - you don't pee in the snow here! Taking souvenirs was forbidden. Throwing stuff overboard was forbidden. No one disagreed with that, but it took time to alter the mindset of at least one cigarette smoker who cast a fag end into the sea when he had finished. If only he could see the number of discarded cigarette ends swallowed by birds, fish, and turtles in their legitimate quest for food.

Stepping ashore on that first day, the childhood memories came flooding back to me. Here I was at last, on the most desolate, most inhospitable, yet beautiful continent on earth. I met some of its inhabitants, a colony of Gentoo penguins. The first thing that hits you when you land at a penguin rookery is the noise, and as you get closer, the smell, a pungent fishy aroma which you soon become accustomed to. Their lavatorial habits are primitive. They squirt a jet of foul-smelling waste from their rear ends, with scant regard for the environment, or any passing neighbour. They are tolerant of humans, and often regarded *us* with as much interest as we had in *them*.

Penguin colony

The two rules when approaching wildlife were: stay at least 5 metres away, and do not stand on a penguin highway. They have their own highways from nest to shoreline, and they are not too pleased to find them blocked. If you stand in their paths they will look at you with a silent gaze that says: 'when are you going to get out of my way?' Delightful to observe, they display a wide range of behaviours on the nest, and as they travel to and from the sea. Both parents take turns on the nest, and hunting for fish underwater.

A couple of immature elephant seals lying side by side, indolent, blubbery masses, raised their heads to watch us, but having decided we were behaving ourselves they settled down to sleep once more.

Some skuas swept low over the rookery, always on the lookout for an unguarded egg or a penguin chick for dinner. Wherever penguins nested, there were skuas menacing from above, or on land where one bird would taunt a parent penguin to get it to move off the nest, while another skua sneaked in from behind to steal the egg. Scattered around the nesting Gentoo penguins were several broken eggshells, evidence of skua predation.

At Dorian Bay, the zodiacs transported us from the ship to another penguin rookery at Damoy Point, and on the way in, I could have sworn I heard the sound of bagpipes. Was this the first sign of polar madness? No. It must be a recording being played on the steel-hulled yacht, Gambo, lying at anchor close to the shore. Wrong again. As we drew closer, I could see a bearded Scot on her deck playing the bagpipes to welcome the expedition team from Explorer to Damoy Point. Gambo's flag proudly bore the Welsh dragon, but she had a mixed crew: a Welshman, an Englishman, an Irishman, an American, and a Scot. Adventurous young men, they were combining cold climate sailing with mountaineering. Two lamb carcasses were strung from the rigging to keep them chilled: the boat's refrigerator was required for the beer.

Once again, it was the kind of night when few people felt like sleeping. A Portuguese guitarist, an American pianist, and myself on harmonica and spoons, held a jam session and provided entertainment in the lounge. The Portuguese radio journalist dashed to her cabin to get her recorder and microphone. To be recorded playing spoons for Portuguese radio was another first for me. It was 2:30 a.m. before I got to bed.

A sunny morning found us anchored off Orne Island. It was the first time the ship had been there and the expedition team had no idea what to expect. They got more than they bargained for. The aim of our exploration of the island was to record the different species of bird, and any other life, we might find. It was a pleasant sunny day, and I chose to wear the kilt ashore. I was greeted with incredulous stares as I waited to embark on the zodiac, but with the temperature soaring to a sweltering five degrees above zero, that would have been regarded as a fine day in Scotland. The island had a good covering of snow, but on several rocky outcrops, small colonies of Chinstrap penguins and skuas nested among the ice-shattered stones. While the penguins were tolerant of our presence, the skuas were not. They mounted diving attacks on the head of anyone who ventured too close to their nesting sites.

The mountain scenery in the background was striking, with saw-toothed ridges, precipitous slopes, and deep snow fields. Large icebergs courted each other as they floated past. With such a backcloth, the sight of a Scot wandering about in a kilt proved too much of an attraction for the TV crew and they asked if they could interview me. Recorded for Portuguese radio the night before, I would now be seen on Portuguese TV as well, wearing the kilt in Antarctica. Better still, every one of the Portuguese ladies insisted on having a photograph taken with the man in the kilt.

Pose for TV Cameras

Neko harbour is a natural haven sheltered by mountains around which glaciers swirled, cracking, and crashing into the sea. The site of a former whaling station and one of the few places with a beach, the only sign of human activity was a hut occasionally used by scientists. The scale of the glacier here can best be seen when viewed from a vantage point high on the hill above. Plodding through knee-deep snow on the climb up to a rocky bluff was not easy, but it was well worth the effort, offering an aerial view of the front of a glacier fissured with crevasses.

Coming down was easier: the slope was so steep all I did was lie on my back in the snow and slide down. I had left the kilt aboard the ship this time and had dressed in conventional polar gear. There *are* limits to what I will do. Lying flat on my back tobogganing downhill - without a toboggan - while wearing a kilt would indeed have been polar madness. That would have brought a flush to my cheeks and the shrinking effect elsewhere doesn't bear thinking about. And the cameras would all have been working overtime! No, I know where to draw the line. Or so I thought.

Having made a rapid descent to the beach, glowing with exhilaration over this childlike pleasure, I caught up with Wendy, a young Australian student teacher. We had spent some time discussing education the day before, an event she had described as 'inspirational.'

"H'y'gan Wendy," I called out in true Australian fashion, "enjoying the expedition?"

"Hi John! Yes, I am. Hey, you've established quite a reputation. I was talking to an American couple today who asked me if I'd met 'that Scotsman who wears a kilt'. They'd been talking with you at lunch, and several other people have mentioned you. You've become a bit of a character. Even the Filipinos in the crew are talking about you."

But what had I done? I began to understand later that night.

CHAPTER 21

As Others See Us

Over two hundred years ago, Scotland's national poet, Robert Burns, in his poem *To A Louse*, expressed the desire 'to see ourselves as others see us.' When it does happen, it can be an arresting experience. I had found the ship warm enough to be able to walk about in a light cotton shirt, tropical shorts, and bare feet, as I had done in the Cook Islands. I kept my cold weather gear for outside. Most of the passengers came on board prepared for the chill winds of Antarctica; woollen sweaters, parkas, woolly hats, and scarves which they continued to wear *inside* the ship. My bare legs and feet attracted incredulous stares.

"Oh, you Scotsmen must be so tough," exclaimed more than one of several admiring women whose gaze followed my athletic, sun-bronzed legs.

"Och aye." I joked. "It's the porridge we eat that keeps us warm." But when I went ashore and trudged through the snow wearing my kilt, my reputation was assured. I was not only tough, but more than a little eccentric as well.

There aren't many beaches in Antarctica, and at our briefing session that evening Wendy had asked Ian, the expedition leader, if there would be an opportunity to have a swim somewhere. Yes. A swim. In the Antarctic Ocean. Among icebergs. During the time we had been there the daily sea temperature had never soared above one degree Celsius, and that was in the mid-day sun. I shook my head. Wendy must have had a wee touch of polar madness. Or maybe not. Students often tend to be a little deranged. I know. I was one once.

Glacier front

Of course, that had been a long time ago, so I had been un-deranged - or so I thought. I hadn't even been daft enough to swim in the sea in Scotland since 1976. The memory of the agonising, throat-constricting shock of icy cold water hitting my chest when I dived in that hot summer had remained with me. I knew what cold water felt like. Those mad enough to want to go swimming were invited to meet with Ian after the briefing. I smiled, the superior smile of the cognoscenti, as I wrapped myself up for an evening excursion into the next bay to observe the wildlife, the glacial scenery, and the icebergs.

We were transported in the zodiacs to a surreal world of spectacular glaciers with caves carved into the pale blue ice walls, great tower blocks of ice leaning drunkenly against each other, and elegant spires soaring heavenwards. And on an ice floe, unimpressed by it all, a large leopard seal lay sleeping.

Normally we think of seals as having cuddly, puppy-like faces with big lovable eyes. The leopard seal does not match this image. These guys are mean. Weighing in at around 500 kg (over 1000 pounds), they have big jaws and a vicious set of teeth. One of the great predators of the sea, they prey on other seals and penguins and have been known to attack humans. A British scientist diving among them was attacked and killed. One of Sir Ernest Shackleton's crew was chased across an ice floe by a leopard seal during the epic voyage in 1916, after their ship, Endurance, had been crushed by ice. As he could run faster, it dived into the sea, swam under the floe and came up again at the other side to confront him. He was saved by the prompt action of one of the crew with a rifle. That was another good argument against going swimming.

We approached this one carefully for photographs. He raised his head once and showed us his teeth. We had no desire to upset him and backed the boat off to observe from a safe distance.

An enormous report like a gunshot echoed around the bay, followed by a thunderous roar - a glacier was calving. We switched our attention to the glacier behind us. It remained unaltered. The calving had occurred around the headland, in the bay where the ship lay at anchor. An enormous wall of ice had crashed into the sea, filling the entire bay with glacial debris. The initial momentum, having scattered the ice well out into the bay, had dissipated, but Explorer was now hemmed in by brash ice, floes, and small icebergs. The zodiacs' engines were not powerful enough to force their way through the mass of floating ice and we were unable to get back to the ship. It was now 10:30 p.m. and we were cold and hungry. The ship's captain called us on the radio. He would operate the bow thruster while still hanging on the anchor and the sideways wash from it would propel the ice floes away from the side of the ship. A gap began to open up, and after about thirty minutes the zodiacs were able to drive through to the ship. Those who had been back aboard earlier had seen it all happening. A wall of ice several hundred metres wide had tumbled into the sea in a domino effect. No one had ever seen anything like it before, not even among the crew, or the expedition team; not even Ian, our expedition leader, an Antarctic junkie on his 79th visit.

The last zodiac arrived - the one with the swimmers. As they climbed back aboard I was met with howls of disbelief. "John! Where were you? Why did you not come for a swim? You're always up for a bit of fun." And this sentiment was echoed by many of the other passengers in the lounge. They were incredulous, the Portuguese in particular. They would have bet good money that I would be leading the charge into the icy waters of the Antarctic. What had happened to me? Had I gone soft?

I was amazed at the reaction. And it wasn't just the passengers - it was the crew too. All my Filipino friends: the boatmen, the stewards, the cleaners looked at me with disappointment written all over their faces. The expedition team, hardened veterans of many Antarctic explorations, also looked stunned: "Oh, you've let us down, John. We thought you would have been the first to volunteer for a dip among the icebergs. We thought you were a hard-as-nails kind of guy who would try anything." Gunther, the German head chef, with whom I had become friends when he was off duty, shook his head in disbelief and turned away to sup his beer, too embarrassed to say anything.

I felt ashamed. Burns's words came back to haunt me. *To see ourselves as others see us.* It was happening to me now. Here I was among people, none of whom I had known a week ago, who saw me as some sort of swashbuckling adventurer, noted for my youthful spirit and hardiness. To them, I was game-for-anything, young-at-heart, John. I thought of all the other things I had done: sailing single-handed in turbulent seas, jungle trekking, kayaking in crocodile infested waters, sky diving, scuba diving, feeding sharks, kissing sting rays (as you do!), swimming in subterranean lakes in limestone caves on remote islands, climbing coconut trees, eating raw sea urchins and the roe of the sea cucumber out on the reef at Rarotonga, trekking kilted through the snowfields of Antarctica… I had been open to new experiences and been enriched by them.

But what had happened to me? I had failed to buckle my swash and lead my followers into the shivering seas. I had constrained myself, denied myself that wonderful euphoria that comes from doing something ridiculous. These people on the ship had admired me, respected me, looked to me for inspiration and leadership. And I had let them down! I crawled off to my cabin and wallowed in black, burning shame.

Before I arose next morning I had resolved to salvage my reputation. Today, I would swim in the icy seas of Antarctica. I sought out Ian, our expedition leader, and put it to him. He looked at me, sat back, and folded his arms. His head tilted to one side.

"How old are you, John?"

"Sixty-three."

He gazed at me: another of his pregnant pauses, a sure sign of disapproval. I did not flinch. He saw the thrawn look in my eye and shrunk before it. "Okay. Tonight." And as I smiled and walked off I heard him mutter, "You're bloody mad."

Maybe. But I was happy to be mad.

And so it came to pass, that at around 10:15 p.m. on the night of January 25, the anniversary of the birth of Robert Burns, I saw myself as others saw me: the bold, fear-nothing adventurer, and three other swimmers joined me. A boat load of spectators from the ship came to see me, as *they* saw me; to record the event on camera, still and video, to show to their incredulous friends back home in the USA, Japan, Korea, Portugal, Norway, or wherever else they came from.

I hadn't wasted the sleepless, shame-filled hours of the night before. I had done some thinking, applied a bit of science to the problem. Thermal shock is caused when the nerve sensors in the body experience a sudden and substantial difference in temperature. I reasoned that if I were able to reduce the temperature differential between my skin and the sea I would experience little shock. In fact the sea temperature would probably be just above the air temperature - at that time of night a degree or two below zero, so it might feel warmer in the water.

Encouraged by that thought, I stripped down to my swimming shorts on the rock. That brought the body temperature down a bit. I began to splash seawater all over my body, spreading it everywhere, into the warm, tender parts. I wanted my skin acclimatised, every blood vessel contracted, every pore tightly closed, every goose pimple standing proud.

The other swimmers jumped in and straight back out again, like one of those film clips when they play it backwards. But I had a reputation to live up to: I went *swimming*. I dived from the rock, headfirst, into the icy sea. My first reaction was one of satisfaction. It wasn't as cold as I had expected. The temperature differential theory was sound. Isn't education a great thing? Exulted, I surged through the water in a gentle upwards sweep, and when my head broke the surface those on the boat gave a resounding cheer. Cameras clicked and whirred and someone called out, "What's it like, John?"

"Boiling!" I retorted. I reckon I'd earned the right to a bit of hyperbole. I swam a few more strokes, smiling, posing for the cameras. Then it hit me. Not a sudden shock like hitting a brick wall: more of a gradual, overpowering, chilling sensation. The intense cold had penetrated deep into my body and I could feel everything contracting, stiffening. I imagined my lungs going solid, my heart being frozen stiff, my blood crystallising. I recalled reading that mariners who fell into the polar seas had only a few minutes to live - if they were fully clothed - and I only had bare skin to protect me. My time was running out. Maybe I only had seconds to live. I won't say I panicked, but I was overcome by a sense of urgency, unique in my lifetime. I swam my fastest-ever front crawl back to that rock. Now, have you ever seen film footage of penguins flying out of the sea and landing feet first on the rocks? Well, that was me that night!

I grabbed my towel and dried the droplets of water before they froze on me, gasping and dancing to get the feeling back into my numbed feet. Then came the most wondrous sensation. Freed from the chilling effect of the sea, the blood vessels in my skin opened up once more and my body glowed with hot blood surging through my arteries, warming my skin. Every atom of my being seemed to exult in this relief. I felt great!

The boatload of spectators was still there, with cameras focused on us as we were getting dressed. Voyeurs! Right, I thought, I'll give the paparazzi something to crow about. I turned my back to them and began to slip my shorts down. Just enough to reveal a hint of posterior cleavage, no more than you can see on any building site when a beer-bellied bricklayer bends over. That got another cheer from the crowd and cries of, "More! More!" I began to dance, a sensuous swaying reminiscent of the Polynesian hula. With my towel wrapped around my waist, I let my shorts slip to my ankles as I writhed and chanted out the tune, The Stripper. The slit in my towel revealed an occasional glimpse of upper thigh, and perhaps a hint of lower left buttock to keep them interested as my shorts dropped to the ground. I flicked my shorts up into the air with my foot, and caught them with my forefinger. I twirled them round and round in the best striptease fashion, then flicked them off my finger and into the crowd who cheered every move. At that point Ian, our leader, called for a halt to this tomfoolery, shaking his head in disbelief. Swimming and a striptease show among the icebergs! What next?

Behind us on the headland, a group of Argentinian scientists at the Cierva Cove research station applauded, and cried out, "Bravo!" We'd had to ask their permission to land and they were out, snug in their thermal long drawers, balaclavas, parkas and mittens, looking on in disbelief. They don't get much entertainment down here. I gave them a departing wave. The boat's engine roared into life, and we raced back to the ship for a hot shower and a warming glass of rum. My reputation had been salvaged.

I had seen myself as others saw me - the real me! Or was it just a bout of polar madness?

CHAPTER 22

Cape Horn

Wilhelmina Bay basked in warm sunshine. Mountains soared out of the sea, their ridges edged with snow cornices. It had a reputation as a good place to see whales, and we were not disappointed. Some orcas and a couple of minkes had been spotted during our voyage, but humpbacks were more in evidence here. Humpback whales, which can grow to lengths of 16 metres (50 feet), are seen in the tropical waters of the Pacific during the breeding season, but migrate south to the nutrient rich waters of Antarctica in the Austral summer. That morning the zodiacs were scattered all over the bay searching for whales.

Cruising towards a mother and her calf, we cut the zodiac's engine and drifted towards them. We got close. Very close. No one spoke. The mother was a mere five metres away, but both she and her calf seemed quite relaxed about our presence. They rested on the surface, looking at us. We looked at them. As mother and calf breathed, fine mists were expelled into the air, and ripples emanating from the rhythmic swelling of their giant bodies ruffled the smooth surface of the sea. We sat motionless, spellbound, inhaling the fishy odour of their breath as it drifted towards us on a windless afternoon, the sun warm on our backs. We were enthralled, hardly daring to breath, lest anything we do might disturb the serenity of the moment. It was more than a moment: we were privileged to commune with these two leviathans for at least twenty minutes. The only sound was the click of cameras.

Humpback whale tail

Underside of tail

One of the other zodiacs had seen us and came roaring over, but cut the engine too late and it drifted too close. They started to back-paddle to 'put the brakes on', but the spell was broken. The mother's back reared up out of the water, the classic hump the prelude to a dive, and like a huge wheel rotating, her body rolled into the sea. The massive tail flukes broke the surface, cascading droplets of water that glowed like diamonds in the sun, and with a final flick she showed us it's scarred underside, the distinctive marks by which, like a fingerprint, each individual whale can be identified. The tail flukes then slipped beneath the surface and she was gone. It was one of my life's most memorable experiences.

On our way back to the ship, the icebergs attracted our attention. The bay had a scattering of large icebergs in a variety of forms: tabular, angular, pyramidal, or in such abstract shapes as to defy description. The oblique light of the early evening sun offered a haunting perspective, highlighting contours, defining areas of light and shadow against the awe-inspiring landscape of windswept snow and ice.

The ship repositioned overnight, taking us to the South Shetland Islands, an impressive archipelago of volcanic origin about seventy miles off the north-west coast of the Antarctic peninsula. Its maritime location ensured a milder climate, with only a few patches of snow. We dropped anchor within a stone's throw of Hannah Point, on Livingston Island. The bay is an ancient volcanic crater with impressive cliff scenery, and in this milder climate the land held patches of moss. The fragility of the environment was again emphasised during our briefing. On no account should we step on the moss as it could take up to a hundred years to recover from the damage caused by one human footprint.

Macaroni Penguin

In terms of wildlife it was the most diverse spot we had yet visited, with noisy chinstrap and gentoo penguin colonies. The penguin chicks were more mature than those we had seen further south, many now developing adult plumage. These colonies attracted attention from kelp gulls, southern sheathbills, skuas, and giant petrels, all intent on finding some food. Another highlight was an elephant seal wallow - there is no more appropriate word to describe it - of young males wallowing on the beach. A few clownish macaroni penguins, easily spotted with their bright yellow, hair-like head feathers, pottered about amongst the chinstraps. Primarily a sub-Antarctic species, only a few Macaroni penguins make it as far south as the peninsula.

While the latitude was similar to that of the Shetland Islands to the north of Scotland, the climate was colder with mid-day temperatures in summer in the range 1 to 6 degrees Celsius. That is comparable to winter mid-day temperatures in the northern Shetland Islands, the climatic difference resulting from the benign effect of the Gulf Stream, or North Atlantic Drift, the warm ocean current that flows from the Gulf of Mexico across the Atlantic Ocean to northern Europe. The warmer sea temperature keeps the ice at bay in the northern latitudes and the warm, moist air it brings maintains a milder, wetter climate all year round. The importance of this natural phenomenon was brought home to me as I surveyed the barren, almost lunar, landscape before me here in the South Shetlands. Apart from a few tufts of tough grass in sheltered spots, only mosses and lichens grow here. Without any depth of soil, there can be no cultivation, no crops, no pasture to support grazing animals. The sea is the only food source. It occurred to me that if, by some whim of nature, the Gulf Stream ceased to flow across the Atlantic Ocean, most of Scotland would become uninhabitable.

That afternoon, we moved to the Aitcho Islands, another scenic archipelago with conspicuous spires of rock soaring out of the sea. The peculiar name Aitcho derives from the British Hydrographic Office initials (H.O.) which once had a base there. The delicate moss beds on Aitcho are among the biggest in the Antarctic, the predominantly green appearance of the island offering a welcome relief after the harshness of rock and ice to which we had become accustomed. These islands support a diverse range of birds and seals, our arrival at the beach being greeted by a cacophony of grunts from a fur seal and a small group of elephant seals. The penguin colonies were by far the largest we had encountered, but with a lesser density of population as they occupied a more spacious and accessible area. Over on the west side, a huge leopard seal lay sleeping at the water's edge close to a penguin colony. The penguins had no fear of him while on land. His cumbersome bulk is not conducive to hunting ashore, but in the sea it is a different matter. Then, sleek as a torpedo, he is just as deadly.

Aitcho Island

Only a few metres from our landing spot, a southern giant petrel and some skuas ripped apart a dead gentoo penguin chick, gorging themselves on its innards. One forlorn looking penguin, the mother, stood around a couple of metres away, making a couple of inept rushes at the scavengers as her chick was ripped apart. No one had seen the kill, but I suspect the chick had become too adventurous and wandered away from its mother's protection. One blow from the feet of a diving skua, or the giant petrel, would easily break its neck. Survival here was a daily struggle.

That evening we left Antarctica and headed north to South America. The wind freshened and by bedtime we were plunging headlong into a full gale. The Drake Passage was living up to its reputation this time. The view from the bridge windows was thrilling. The ship shuddered as she smashed her bows into each wave, spray lashing the wheelhouse windows. Cape Horn lay ahead. The captain took us to the west of the cape and then ran eastwards past it at 5 a.m. Visibility was poor so we could only see a dark mass of rock in the murky, grey light of a dismal morning, but I suppose that is how Cape Horn appears to most people who have sailed these waters. I crawled back into my bunk again with my thoughts.

I felt privileged to be included in the select band of people who have been 'Round the Horn' in a gale, a place that I had read about in books in my childhood and youth when I consumed stories of the sea in bucketfuls. I had been to Antarctica, the most remote place on earth, the only continent whose permanent human population is 0. Its temporary inhabitants number just a few hundred scientists, with a few summer tourists, on a continent about one and a half times the size of the United States of America. It has been estimated that in just under two hundred years since Antarctica was discovered, no more than 250,000 people have ever set foot on it - and I was one of them.

Our final night aboard the ship was spent tied up in harbour at Ushuaia. When some of the Filipino crew came off watch that night they insisted that I join them for a run ashore: "You always take the time to talk with us, Sir John, so we want to buy you a drink before you leave."

They took me to the Irish Pub. Along with Coca Cola and McDonald's, you will find Irish Pubs all over the world. The Filipinos were interested in knowing where else I had been on my travels and one of the stewards asked me, "Why don't you come to the Philippines?"

I told him I had been thinking of visiting the Philippines, having been impressed by the friendliness of the boys in the crew and the girls who tended the cabins. I had also heard a positive report of the Philippines from a German I had met in the Cook Islands who assured me I would find very good diving there.

The steward beamed. "Come and stay, John. You would have a nice warm climate, the scuba diving is very good, and it is a cheap place to live. You could live comfortably on your pension. Marry a nice Filipina and she will take good care of you."

"Och, I am too old for that now. No Filipina would want to marry an old guy like me."

"No, no, John. You are never too old. Age doesn't matter in the Philippines. I see you talking with the girls on the ship. They like you. I'm sure you would have no problem finding a nice Filipina who would want to marry you. You would be a very attractive prospect as a husband."

Mmm… ? Tropical islands, cheap living, excellent diving in warm seas, caring maidens willing to look after me. What more could a man want? Maybe I should include the Philippines in the itinerary for my next trip around the world.

Whether my visit to Antarctica was a life changing experience for me is debatable. It is perhaps best considered as one among many influences. My son once wrote in response to an email account of my antics in the Cook Islands: 'Who is this guy we are reading about? Or maybe I should be asking who is the person we see here in Scotland? Which one is the real you?'

Was I really so different? Behaviour is a function of environment, and while the physical environment may stimulate, challenge, induce a sense of relaxation, or give cause for thought, the interaction with people has a more profound effect. Behaviour can be influenced by the expectations of others and how they perceive you. The pressure I felt to swim among the icebergs was a good example. Such expectations may be determined by preconceptions, or the power of stereotypes. Watch people when a dog comes into their presence. If the dog approaches wagging its tail, people are more likely to react in a positive manner towards it, yet some may still recoil in fear, a response to their own prejudices. How the dog is received, whether accepted or rejected, will determine its behaviour thereafter. In my home community I am defined as father, grandfather, retired headmaster - all roles with attendant stereotypical expectations. Perhaps it is more difficult to shake off the burden of expectation in the local environment, but while travelling, these constraints don't apply as the people you meet are unlikely to have the same expectations of you.

It would be difficult to claim any one place in all my travels has changed me, although perhaps my first visit to the Cook Islands was a particularly formative experience. That was my real initiation into the backpacking community: a sort of loose brotherhood with few barriers, few stereotypes, where age doesn't seem to matter so much. Maybe one day I will have 'found myself,' but I see life as more of a process, of continued development, a response to whatever environment I happen to inhabit at any given time, in which youth is less a function of age and more a function of the learning process in relation to whatever we want to do. At present, I am still only 'seeing through a glass darkly,' but seeing myself through the eyes of others has been an illuminating experience.

My naivety and innocence as a traveller have dissipated. Through a variety of experiences I have learned a great deal, and I now feel I am no longer a 'virgin' backpacker.

On the flight back to Buenos Aires from Ushuaia, I reflected upon the events of the last few months. It was galling to have lost all the photos I had taken from the start of my round the world trip to the day my camera and computer had been stolen at Buenos Aires. But they could be replaced. I was alive, I was fit, and I could travel again. It was imperative that I return to Easter island, allowing myself more time there to take photos. I could then island-hop westwards across the Pacific to the Cook Islands, and move on to some other good diving locations. A plan was forming in my mind.

I spent a few days in Brazil with my nephew and his wife, and on the flight back to London I planned my next trip. London to Easter Island is a long way, but I could stop in Ecuador to explore the Galapagos Islands, on land and underwater. Flying from Ecuador to Chile would connect me with the flight from Santiago to Easter Island. I would spend more time there: enough to recapture all the photos, and more, and experience the social life of the island. From there I could hop over to the Cook Islands for another spell of voluntary work, then take the chief steward's advice about visiting the Philippines. Apart from changing flights at Singapore, I had never been to any of the countries of South-East Asia, but that was about to change - and my lifestyle with it.

CHAPTER 23

Galapagos Islands

M y eye surveyed a barren, lunar landscape of volcanic ash and lava flows pock-marked with a scattering of spatter cones, the small craters around the slopes of the volcanic cone on which I stood, where hot gases had forced their way out before the crust had cooled. But I was not on the moon. I've been about a bit, but I am not that far travelled - yet.

Bartholeme Island

Far below where I stood, our boat, *Galapagos Adventurer III*, lay at anchor in a bay that was once the caldera of an ancient volcano that had blown itself apart, leaving only one remnant still proud of the ocean: a conical pillar standing sentinel at one end of a sandy bay. This iconic view of Bartholeme Island is one of the most spectacular in the Galapagos Islands.

A group of 18 volcanic islands, only five of which are inhabited, the Galapagos Islands lie about 1000 km (600 miles) west of Ecuador. Although they straddle the equator, they have a temperate climate due to the cold water Humboldt Current which sweeps up the west coast of South America from the Antarctic. This is moderated by the Panama current, bringing warm water from the north, while the Cromwell undercurrent from the west brings nutrient-rich water from the depths of the Pacific Ocean.

The result is a unique marine environment teeming with fish: whale sharks, hammerheads and several other varieties of shark, manta rays, turtles, schools of devil rays flying past like squadrons of delta-winged aircraft, the biggest sting rays I had ever seen, spotted eagle rays, as well as a host of smaller fish. The diversity of the marine life is astonishing. Sea lions, abundant in such fish-filled waters, delight in joining divers and copying their actions, blowing bubbles in imitation of the discharge of air from the diver's regulator. Playful as puppies, they will come right up close and peer through your mask, looking into your eyes. You could fall in love with these animals.

On land, you can walk among the hundreds of disinterested marine iguanas that litter the coastline as they bask in the sun to increase their body heat, statuesque relics from the dinosaur age. Further inland you can find the larger land iguanas lazing around, their natural camouflage making it difficult to spot them until you are among them.

The birds here show no fear of man. The visitor may wander among their nests where they sit without concern. The courtship displays of the frigate birds are remarkable, the males puffing up the large, red, balloon-like sacks located under their beaks in order to attract the females. Waved albatrosses perform a mating dance, with a loud clacking of beaks as they 'fence' with each other, followed by a vociferous celebration as they recognise each other as mates. Blue-footed boobies and Nazca Boobies (birds of the gannet family) are also found in abundance. Galapagos hawks will pose fearlessly on scrub vegetation, allowing the photographer to come near for close-up pictures of the fearsome looking beak and eagle eyes. Tidal lagoons are home to elegant pink flamingoes, brown pelicans and the many small waders that feed there. The lava flows are populated with brilliant red, orange, yellow and blue patterned sally-lightfoot crabs which dance across the black surface of the lava, quite happy to investigate a bare foot if one stood still.

Marine Iguana

Land Iguana

Frigate Bird

Blue-footed Booby

Flamingo   Brown Pelican

It is astonishing to find penguins on islands straddling the equator. The Galapagos Penguin is the only species of penguin to be found in the northern hemisphere. The equator passes through Isabella island, one of their habitats, so they can be seen on both sides of the equator there. For anyone interested in observing wildlife, this is a naturalist's and photographer's dream.

Galapagos landscapes can be surreal. Some islands, like Bartholeme Island, are young, mere infants in geological terms, but they grow with each successive volcanic eruption. On such arid landscapes, the earliest drought-resistant pioneer plants are only now beginning to take hold. They will add humus to the mineral rich soil as their leaves fall. The leaves will compost to provide more moisture-retentive soil, and that will allow other plants and trees to establish themselves. Some of the older islands, (estimated at around a mere three million years) have desert-like vegetation along the arid low ground near the coast, but the higher level of precipitation in the mountains results in lush vegetation. This is the home of the giant tortoises from which the islands get their name, many weighing over 100 kilos (250 lbs). They munch the vegetation and have a particular liking for the succulent young opuntia (prickly pear) cactus.

Giant Tortoise

Human habitation has only a brief history among the wonderland of wildlife of the Galapagos, hence their lack of fear of man. Discovered in 1535 by the Archbishop of Panama, whose ship was becalmed and drifted for several days until, almost out of water, he was saved from extinction when the Galapagos Islands appeared. It then became a pirates' lair, a source of food and fresh water, well placed for plundering the Spanish galleons laden with riches from the west coast of Mexico. It proved a popular stop for whalers in the 18th and 19th centuries. They too could replenish food and water supplies. These short-term visitors laid waste to the wildlife: hundreds of thousands of birds, tortoises, and turtles were plundered for food. It was just too easy.

In 1793 an enterprising British whaler, Captain James Colnett, allegedly established the 'Galapagos Post Office' - a wooden barrel - which exists to this day in what has become known as Post Office Bay on Floreana Island. Outward bound whalers dropped off mail and homeward bound ships picked it up and delivered it to whatever country they were bound for. It is now used by tourists as a unique way to get postcards home without having to pay postage, although it may take a long time before someone from your particular locality, homeward bound, arrives on the scene to deliver it. Although a penal colony had been established in the late 19th century, it was only in the early years of the 20th century that real settlement began. The 2010 Census recorded a population of about 25,000 spread over five of the islands.

One name that will be forever linked with the Galapagos islands is Charles Darwin, the young English naturalist who arrived here in 1835 on the survey ship HMS Beagle. His observations and biological collections inspired much of the thinking that led to his theories of natural selection and evolution, published in his Earth-stirring (and in the opinion of some, notorious) treatise The Origin of Species, which rocked the scientific and religious communities in the 19th century - and still creates controversy between religious creationists and scientific thinkers.

My voyage of exploration in the Galapagos was arranged under the auspices of Gap Adventures, the Canadian based adventure travel company with whom I had enjoyed exploring the mountains of Patagonia and Antarctica. Galapagos Adventurer III, a comfortable boat carrying 16 passengers, dropped us off at various locations for exploration of this unique environment under the care of an approved guide. Tourism is strictly controlled, with just under 3% of the Galapagos area approved for human activity to minimise the harmful effects on the environment. Only boats carrying small groups of tourists are allowed. My tour included the option of diving, as well as exploring on land. That is no longer allowed. You must now either dive without any land-based exploration, or explore on land without any diving.

On the day Ecuador was playing Uruguay in a football world cup qualifying match, we had a run ashore on Santa Cruz. The streets were almost deserted, but you could hear the sound of the match on TV from every shop and bar, and everyone was decked out in the bright yellow colours of Ecuador. When the final whistle blew, the result was in Ecuador's favour and the town went mad. Cars and motorbikes drove around in cavalcades, blowing horns and waving flags. Music and dancing took over, all along the streets. Passing an open-air café, I glanced towards a waitress who was dancing solo, her yellow shirt and blue jeans complimenting each other perfectly. As I gazed in admiration, her eyes met mine and her hands, in perfect time to the music, beckoned me towards her.

Now, I really don't know how I get sucked into these things. I wasn't even wearing the kilt on that occasion, so I don't know why she picked *me* from the crowds of passers-by. Maybe I just looked irresistibly handsome, or perhaps she was attracted to my moderately proportioned, but athletic physique. Perhaps I exuded a pheromone laden magnetism - or maybe I am just a hopeless fantasist!

Whatever the reason, it would have been alien to my gentlemanly characteristics to refuse such an invitation and, well, her hips did move in the most delectable fashion. So I joined her, my hips swivelling in unison with hers.

I had just 'met a girl called Maria' and in this real-life blend of South Pacific and West Side Story we danced like star-crossed lovers. We improvised creatively, sometimes apart, sometimes holding each other close, gazing into each other's eyes. At the end, cheers of "Bravo" and "Encore" erupted from the watching crowd. I had no objection, and Maria was more than willing to get to grips with me again.

The Galapagos islands' unique wildlife and landscapes have an enormous 'Wow' factor. It is like nowhere else on earth. I would love to go back again.

What a pity I didn't get Maria's phone number!

CHAPTER 24

Unforgettable

It was one of those unforgettable moments. I had been dragged out at mid-night (social activities only start at mid-night in Easter Island) to go dancing with Joanna, my host's daughter, and her cousin, Oscar. This was an element of Easter Island social life I had missed on my previous visit. It was a 'must do,' according to Joanna. They led me to a bar where the sound of a string band, six guitars and a drummer, drifted out into the warm night air. The door of the bar was like the swing doors in the old western movies.

"You go in first, John,' said Joanna.

I looked over the top of the swing doors. On my right were several tables with people sitting at them. At the end of the room was a low platform on which the band played. A few couples danced. To the left of the band was the bar, crowded three or four deep with leathery-skinned macho men swilling their beer. Now, when you live in just about the most remote island community in the world and a Scotsman walks through the door, kilt swinging, I suppose it does have an element of surprise.

A tsunami of silence swept through the room.

Hands froze: guitar strings twanged their last twang. The drum stopped beating. The dancers stopped dancing. The talkers stopped talking. The drinkers stopped drinking, glasses held halfway to their lips, mouths gaping open, eyes wide in astonishment. Everyone froze.

Except me.

I took a deep breath.

"Brazen it out," I told myself. "Set your shoulders, and swing that kilt."

I walked towards the bar with measured pace, one step per second (just like in the movies) click...click...click, the steel-tipped heels of my sturdy brogues resounding on the wooden floor. It was like being the head of a school again, walking with that undisputed air of authority into the assembly hall and the whole school goes quiet, waiting for words from the cousin of God. The set of the shoulders, the powerful, measured step, the swing of the kilt sent out a message: "Nothing will stop me."

The men were clustered around the bar, but I was going to part them, like Moses raising his staff at the waters of the Red Sea, by the sheer power of my presence.

What a marvellous thing is faith! And would you believe it? It worked. I never faltered in my step and all those red-necks with their cowboy hats on, opened up and let me through. The last man, sitting on a bar stool, jumped up, and with a flourish, beckoned me on to his stool. Not a word was spoken. I turned to see Joanna and Oscar a few steps behind me.

"What are you drinking?" I asked them.

"No ningún, déjeme le consiguen una bebida!" exclaimed the man who had offered me his seat. They speak Spanish here.

I hadn't a clue what he had said, but the barmaid asked me, "Beer? He's buying."

She had one already in her hand, poured for another customer. It never reached him. She placed it in front of me. I had VIP status.

I raised my glass, looked around the silent gathering as still they gazed and still the wonder grew, nodded, and said, "Slainthe Mhath!" the traditional Scottish toast: 'good health'. They all smiled, and raised their glasses in acknowledgement. I looked at the band. They were all smiling too. I smiled back and nodded. They struck up again and the party took off once more.

Men crowded round to shake my hand and talk. Behind them I could see a woman eyeing me up: a willowy, wild-looking creature with flashing eyes, part Chilean, part Polynesian, probably with a bit of Spanish from a few generations back. Must be an artist, I thought, by the look of her. I found her a lot more interesting to look at than the men, and as she seemed interested in looking at me, I smiled at her. It was all the encouragement she needed. She wriggled through the throng, pushing the macho men aside. I held out my hand and she took it. Then she took both my hands in hers and held them apart. She looked me up and down, appraising me with her artist's eye for colour, shape and form. Her eyes flashed their appreciation.

"Oooooh..... you are so beeyoooootiful!"

"Och aye, I know," and I reciprocated the compliment: "You're no' bad lookin' yersel'." I just can't stop the intoxicating poetry that flows from my lips.

There must be something powerful about the Scottish propensity for understatement when expressing compliments to a lady. It seemed to have a Pheromone Effect, for she then dragged me out of the crowd and on to the dance floor, where our bodies swayed in harmony to the music and the band smiled their approval.

When the music stopped, I got no more than two or three steps back towards the bar before another woman pounced on me and dragged me away from Angela (we had introduced ourselves by this stage, whispering our names into each other's ears as we danced). She claimed possession of me for the next dance. And that is how it went on all night, one woman after another. Wives abandoned husbands, girlfriends propped boyfriends up at the bar with a glass of beer to keep them amused, while they had their way with me on the dance floor. I never had to make a move on any of them.

It was 6:30 a.m. when Joanna and Oscar hauled me away from the clutches of yet another amorous woman. Her English was non-existent, but her body language was unambiguous. I think Joanna was concerned that my austere Presbyterian sense of denial might crumble and yield to temptation after more than six hours relentless onslaught by the wild women of Rapa Nui, so she and Oscar dragged me home. Spoilsports!

I recalled another of Joanna's cousins telling me on my previous visit, "You could get up to some mischief wearing that kilt at a dance here." She was right too. I could have, but for the attentions of my chaperones.

Easter Island, Rapa Nui in the local language, or Isla de Pascua in Spanish, is a UNESCO world heritage site and ranks alongside the Galapagos Islands, the Great Barrier Reef etc as one of the most treasured places on Earth. It is one of the most fascinating and atmospheric places I have visited.

My last visit of four days was not nearly enough. This time I stayed for ten and my aim was to recapture all the photographs that had been stolen with my laptop in Buenos Aires. The quality of light in the mornings and evenings was ideal for photography when the low angle of the sun presented light and shade and a mellow colour. This meant rising early to get to the sites, or delaying till late afternoon.

This time I had the opportunity to explore the strange stone houses at Orongo, at the top of the volcanic crater of Rano Kau, near the one town on the island, Hanga Roa. It seems odd that people should want to build low stone dwellings high up on the edge of a crater where, on one side, the land fell off into the crater, now full of stinking, sulphurous water, while on the other side a fearsome cliff dropped to the sea about 300 metres below. But that is only one of many enigmatic things about Easter Island. While the Moai and their history are the main attraction on the island, there are many other interesting features.

Many of the rocks have petroglyphs, strange carvings related to the cult of the bird-man. Each year the young men swam in competition to a small rocky island off the western tip of Easter Island where the Sooty Tern nested. Braving the strong currents that ran between it and the main island, the first man to return with an egg of the sooty tern became the bird-man for the year. No one was allowed to touch him. Food was brought to him. He lived in isolation on the top of the crater rim and was regarded as a Demi-God. It doesn't sound like much fun, but it was a prestigious role to play for a year.

I also had time to explore the many caves along the shoreline that had once been the refuge of the inhabitants. Some of these had paintings on their walls. Life for the islanders did not seem to be very comfortable back then.

Easter Island is a haunting sort of place and begs more questions than it answers, but perhaps it issues a very clear warning to us all regarding the over-exploitation of the environment. Here is a powerful message indeed, pointing to the devastation of a community as a result of blind adherence to a particular dogma. As described in chapter 16, we cannot rape our natural environment without serious consequences. In that respect, Easter Island is a monument to man's folly.

I enjoyed ten energetic days with hikes up volcanoes, or bouncing around in a jeep across the rough and dusty island roads. One guidebook offered two classifications for the roads: indescribable, and unspeakable.

The arrival of the thrice-weekly flights from Santiago or Tahiti is always a cause for ceremony and visitors are welcomed at the airport with garlands of flowers draped over their shoulders, a regular Polynesian custom. While taking photos of this aspect of Rapa Nui life, a lady appeared at my shoulder. It was Angela, who had been my first dancing partner on that first evening out. She seemed delighted to see me again. We agreed to meet for lunch to catch up with what I had been doing; an interesting event as we conversed in several different languages, improvising and switching from one to another to find the right words, with a bit of sign language thrown in. She spoke the native Rapa Nui language, Spanish, French, and German, but had only a little English. I spoke English with a little French and German, no Spanish, but a little Rapa Nui, which is basically the same Polynesian language that is spoken with variations in Tahiti, Cook Islands, and Hawaii. It is amazing how you can overcome the communication difficulties if you are creative.

Afterwards she took me to her cabana, a house she lets out to visitors. Of a unique design - she had designed and built it with her own hands - it was the kind of house that only an artist could have built. She asked me if I would take some photos of it to include in promotional brochures to be sent to prospective customers. I shot some pictures, processed them on the laptop, and then we worked on a layout for the brochures and got them printed. She then went off to chip away all night at a sculpture she was working on and I felt satisfied that I had done something which may have been of some economic benefit to this remote community in the vastness of the Pacific Ocean.

Joanna, my host's daughter, then press-ganged me into helping out with her husband and Oscar on her small farm. She sat on the horse driving it up and down the field while her husband walked behind, guiding the single-furrow plough. She grows pineapples, watermelons, peaches, taro, and some other vegetables. I helped with the planting and hoeing the weeds around the peach trees. Like helping out on the croft back home, it was a communal effort to get the work done while the weather was suitable. That evening we dined by candlelight in the farm kitchen. It had no electricity or plumbed water, only rainwater, and that night there was plenty of it. We slept on mattresses on the floor, while a thunderous downpour watered in the vegetables we had planted. It was a taste of the simple life; a satisfying experience.

Easter Island is such a remote community that most visitors come only once. However, my return to Easter Island proved to be an even more enriching experience than the first visit. Walking along the road at any time, day or night, it was a common occurrence for taxis to stop, the driver calling out, "Hey Escosia! Weelliam Wallace!" Thanks to the film, Braveheart, everyone knew about William Wallace, the 13th century Scottish patriot whose guerrilla struggles against the imperialist English king have become the stuff of legend. This is something the people of Rapa Nui can identify with, having been annexed by Chile in 1888. Many of the drivers stopped to talk with me, and the passengers did not seem to mind in the slightest. Some local girls asked permission to have photographs taken with me, snuggling up close. I stoically endured it all without complaint.

A local girl I met at the airport astonished me when she told me she lived in Scotland with her fiancé. When I asked where, she replied, "Oh, it is only a small town. You have probably never heard of it."

"Try me."

"Kilwinning."

I laughed. "I was born only three miles from there, in Irvine."

She was back on her home island for a few months, driving a taxi to earn some money, and her fiancé was coming out for a month at Christmas.

So many people seemed to know me in such a short time there and the night before I left, while having dinner with Angela, I remarked on the friendliness shown to me everywhere I went. She nodded. "Si, everybody in Rapa Nui know you, John. Many people tell me about you."

"But why?"

"Mmmm… you très sympaticos. Touristos come, look at moai, go. But you make *connection*. You help Joanna with farm, help me take photos for brochure. You work with us, dance with us, speak with us on the street."

I reflected on her words, especially on that important word: connection. Am I emitting some subliminal signal of need, subconsciously seeking to connect? I reflected on the question I have been asked many times, "Why are you travelling, John?" I don't know, but it is curious how I get drawn into things. How I seem to *connect*.

The mantle of tourist does not fit well with me. Tourist is too passive a description. When people ask if I am on holiday, I shake my head. I don't see it as such. I regard it as an itinerant lifestyle, wandering the world, learning from the people I meet, sometimes being able to offer something. This may be overt, like helping Joanna on the family farm, or with Angela's brochure, but at other times it may not be a conscious act at all.

On the day I left, Joanna's mother, Theresa, who owned the guesthouse, surprised me by telling me my visit had helped her. Her husband had died after I had left Easter Island on my previous visit. My return had meant much to her, she told me, knowing that I had experienced the loss of my wife.

"You help me so much, John," she told me. "Every morning you come for breakfast, you are always so cheerful. You talk with me. You make me laugh. This is good for me. I miss my husband so much, but you show me the way. I try to follow your example. Try to be positive. I never forget you, John."

Through the example of lifestyle, a personal response to my own bereavement, and particularly in maintaining a positive outlook, I was unwittingly offering something significant to someone in need. We should never underestimate the importance of the apparently mundane things we do and how our example may impinge on the lives of others. Our lives are shaped by a complex series of interactions. Somehow, I felt I too had been granted something special from the Rapa Nui people. They made me laugh, made me feel cherished, respected, and this fuelled any positive outlook I managed to maintain, but it is not always easy. I still have my bad times when I can plunge into grim moods, but the interactions with the people I meet on my travels pull me out of gloom.

On my arrival at the airport to check-in my luggage, the three check-in clerks stood up simultaneously, raised their fists in salute and cried out, "Weelliam Wallace." I burst out laughing. It was as though they had been rehearsing it for my arrival. I shook hands with them, said my goodbyes, then I waited for a while before going through security into the departure lounge because Angela had said she would see me at the airport before I left.

As departure time approached, I gave up. Typical Polynesian, I thought, no concept of time. I went through security and joined the crowd in the departure lounge. With only a few minutes left before boarding, I heard a cry: "John!" I turned round and there was Angela, rushing past the security guard to give me a final hug and say goodbye, and thank me for helping her with the brochure. She had even managed to talk her way through the security gates to get to me! Well, it is only a small island where everyone is known and rules are tolerated rather than slavishly obeyed, another aspect of island life that I liked.

But she wasn't the last to say goodbye. Walking over the tarmac to the aircraft I heard a voice call, "John!" One of the ground crew, working under the wing, was waving to me. "You leaving now, John?"

"Yes," I called back, and gave him a wave. I climbed the steps to the aircraft door and took one final look back. With military precision, he stood to attention and raised his arm in a crisp salute. I had to smile. My hand shot up to acknowledge his salute. We held our salutes to each other for a couple of seconds. I lowered my hand, and only then did he lower his. His face cracked in a big grin and he called out, "Goodbye, John."

I turned into the aircraft and felt a wave of sadness on leaving this enigmatic island and its friendly people. Angela's words, as she slipped into French in our final conversation, echoed my sentiments: "Quelle domage tu depart."

"What a pity you are leaving."

CHAPTER 25

Surprise Encounters

T he flight from Easter Island to Tahiti took about five hours, arriving around 11p.m. I had a five-hour wait to connect with the flight from Los Angeles to Rarotonga, arriving there around 6 a.m. At the immigration desk, the officer looked up and smiled. "Papa John! You have come back home!" That touched me.

Adrienne, the manager of Tiare Village Hostel, was at the airport to welcome me. Two other guests from the same flight were already waiting beside her. She introduced us.

"Papa John, this is Mike and Susan." As we shook hands she told them, "If you need to know anything about Rarotonga, Papa John is the man to ask."

"Papa John!" exclaimed Mike. "You mean, *the* Papa John?"

"Yes, that's him," laughed Adrienne.

I looked bemused. "You've heard of me?"

"You're famous! I read about you on the internet. Someone wrote about this Scottish guy called Papa John who loves Rarotonga, comes every year, wears a kilt, guides them through the jungle, shows them where to snorkel, and offers help and advice. Reading that persuaded me to come here." It was gratifying to know that I was contributing to the promotion of tourism in the Cook Islands.

That night, we all went to the traditional dance show. After the show had finished a young man approached me and spoke with a Scottish accent.

"I didnae expect tae see a kilt in Rarotonga. Whit's the tartan?"

"McMillan."

"I'm a MacLean." His accent intrigued me.

"Where are you from?"

"Kilmarnock."

"I thought you sounded familiar. I was born in Irvine." (Only 7 miles from Kilmarnock)

"Oh, my father was born in Irvine."

"Your father? Would that be Donald MacLean, graduated BSc in mechanical engineering, Glasgow University, 1961?"

"Aye!" he gasped, "You know him?"

"Know him? We went to the same primary and secondary schools, the same church and Sunday school, we were in the Boys Brigade together, and we both went to Glasgow University. Not only that, we're related. Your great-great-grandmother was a sister of my great-grandfather, so your great-great-great-grandfather is our common ancestor."

His jaw dropped. "Bloody Hell! You come half way round the world to a tiny island in the middle of the Pacific Ocean and you meet a distant relative and get half your family tree! I can't wait to tell my Dad about this."

His wife brought out a camera. "We'll have to take a picture of you both and email it to him. This is almost beyond belief."

Now, if I hadn't been wearing the kilt, that family union would never have taken place. It always attracts people.

One Sunday I had gone with a group from the hostel to the church in Avarua to listen to the marvellous singing. We always sat in the balconies on either side, but as we stood up for the first hymn I noticed a couple, obviously visitors, sitting in the pews below. The man looked up around the balconies, but his gaze was arrested when he saw me wearing the kilt. His face looked familiar.

As we left the church, we met at the doorway. "I got such a shock when I looked up and saw a kilt on Rarontoga," he said. "What tartan is that?"

"McMillan." I said, "John." I held out my hand.

"Alasdair." He shook my hand and introduced me to his wife.

"What brings you to Rarotonga?" I asked.

"Just stopping for a few days to break the journey home after visiting our daughter in New Zealand. And you?"

"I'm doing some voluntary work in schools for a few months."

"So you were a teacher in Scotland?" And when he learned I had been head of Invergordon Academy he said, "You'll know Ewen Stewart then." Ewen had been head of the music department in the school.

"Of course. How do you know him?"

"He invited me to come and sing for the Invergordon Arts Society many years ago."

And then it dawned on me. I was talking with Alasdair Gillies, a popular singer who regularly appeared on Radio and TV in Scotland in the 1960s and 1970s.

Fast forward 20 years...I was at Eden Court Theatre in Inverness watching a tribute to Fergie MacDonald, whose music I had used to teach the Cook Islands kids to do Scottish dances. The first person to come on to the stage to talk about his acquaintance with Fergie was Alasdair. They had started their careers on TV on the same show. At the interval, he joined the audience to watch the rest of the show and sat beside his wife, who was sitting in the row behind me. I turned around and said, "Hello again, Alasdair."

He looked at me for a moment. "I know your face from somewhere…"

"Remember the Kirk on Rarotonga?"

"The man in the kilt! From Invergordon. You were working in the schools there and teaching the kids Scottish dances. Look, don't leave at the end. We must get together and talk."

We chatted for some time afterwards and he invited me to visit him any time I was in the Glasgow area. Aye, you can't beat the kilt for making friends.

CHAPTER 26

Jigs & Reels

After Ronan Martin, a sailing friend from the Isle of Skye, Scotland, and a skilled fiddler and piper, arrived on Rarotonga, there had been little rest. I had last seen him one stormy weekend at the end of August as our boats sheltered from a gale at the Isle of Rona. He told me he was planning a tour of Australia and New Zealand in November and December and I suggested that he should come to Rarotonga. He had brought the fiddle, but left the bagpipes at home as he wanted to travel light.

With the fiddle and the spoons we performed on a Friday night at The Staircase Restaurant, introducing some traditional Scottish music to the audience, who tapped their feet, nodded heads, and clapped their hands in time to the music. It was the same at the Sailing Club on the Saturday. We took part in the afternoon's racing, slicing through the turquoise waters of a lagoon fringed with three small tree-covered islands and a ribbon of white where the Pacific breakers crashed on the reef. Along the shore, swaying palms cast dappled shadows over white coral sand - I get delirious thinking about it. A barbecue followed the racing, and we followed the barbecue with some toe-tapping jigs, strathspeys, and reels. That was a surprise for most of the club members who had no idea what was in store for them, but they loved it.

On the Sunday night we played at the poolside at the hostel for a group of people who had come over from New Zealand for a clan gathering of the Cowans, all descended from a virile Scot who arrived here in the 1880s and married two Cook Islanders - but not simultaneously. His first wife died after giving him six children and he had about the same number with his second wife. His offspring went forth and multiplied across the South Pacific and his descendants were now coming back to Rarotonga from Australia, New Zealand, Tahiti, Tonga, Samoa, and several of the Cook Islands to the place where it all started. This group enjoyed the music, and when they met several more relatives who were staying at other places on the island, they asked us if we would perform again on the Monday night for them.

This time we taught them to dance Strip the Willow, a lively Scottish dance. The intricate movements of the dance gave rise to a fair bit of confusion, but they were game for a laugh and we all had great fun. They had more of the same on the Wednesday afternoon, when we played at the Clan Gathering of the South Pacific Cowans.

Ronan had also been invited to join the band with whom I had been playing every week at the Whatever Bar. While the band played Cook Island songs, Ronan improvised, providing beautifully crafted harmonies to accompany the guitars and ukeleles. Then he and I played some Scottish jigs and reels that got the feet tapping and hands clapping, and with Ronan calling out key changes, the guitar and ukelele players demonstrated their versatility by joining in with a powerful rhythm section.

Steve, better known by his nickname, Moko, was the leader of the band. He played with one of the professional dance team bands, was a former Cook Islands male Dancer of the Year, and was keen to have us stick around for a while longer to work out some arrangements.

However, the heat and humidity affected the glue that held the neck to the body of Ronan's fiddle and it came apart a few days before he had to fly back to New Zealand. He found a boatbuilder who was also a musician and had a stock of glues. He was an English-born ex-Royal Navy helicopter pilot, now a naval architect, who enjoyed life on the island, inventing things and designing innovative small craft such as a solar-powered lagoon boat. With Ronan also being a professional designer, sailor, and musician they had plenty in common to talk about. They glued on the neck and left the fiddle clamped overnight, but the glue couldn't take the strain when the strings were tensioned.

That ruled Ronan out of our proclaimed return performance at the Whatever Bar, advertised in the Cook Island News with typical tongue-in-cheek humour, 'Resident band with guest stars, featuring some of the world's best musicians.'

It was disappointing for the music lovers that Ronan was ruled out and I was the only 'guest star' performing. That left us with a line up of three ukeleles, two guitars and the spoons. Steve, the bandleader, introduced me. "Please welcome our special guest star and spoon player, John, our cousin from Scotland, to play for you tonight." That brought a round of applause. They looked pleased to see me - even those who'd sat through all the previous weeks' performances. He carried on, "We claim John as our cousin because we have shared a common ancestor. His great-great-grandfather came to the Cook Islands in the 1820s - and we ate him! John has been playing with us for about two months now - and he is still single!" He shook his head and gave me a pathetic look. "So if any of you ladies are looking for a husband, he's available and needs a good Cook Island woman to take care of him." Steve's cheeky humour always brought smiles - and even a few offers of matrimony!

He added that the band would be happy to perform any requests from the audience. "Just ask us. We know all the songs. We may not know all the words, but we know all the songs. And please, order more drinks from the bar. That will make the management happy, and the more you drink, the better we sound."

Later on, he introduced a bit of unscheduled cabaret. One of the regular patrons, Sylvia, a stunning girl with a great sense of fun, was also a princess, a daughter of the king of Mauke, one of the outer islands. Moko, in his usual cheeky manner, insisted that she should dance for us while the band played and sang a song from Mauke. After much shaking of her head, she gave in to cheers of encouragement from the audience and performed a beautiful slow dance. Moko followed that by calling for her friend, Kura, a girl from Mitiaro, to accompany a Mitiaro song. She performed too. Then he called on a Tahitian girl who came up and sang a Tahitian song. By this time it had become a right *ceilidh*, the kind of impromptu social gathering with music and dancing that is traditional in the highlands and islands of Scotland.

To follow that, Moko announced that it was time for an Ura Peani, the Cook Island dance for the Europeans to try, and called on Sylvia to partner an Australian from the audience who had just become engaged. He gave a commendable and enthusiastic rendition of Cook Islands style dancing, but to my surprise, Moko took my spoons from me and announced, "And now Johnnie from Scotland will demonstrate how Cook Islands dancing should be done… and Kura will partner him."

I'd never met Kura before. "Kia Orana," I greeted her in the usual fashion with a kiss on the cheek. The music started. I like the look of surprise when I dance with someone who doesn't know me. My knees got going, arms stretched out in front, hands working an invitation. She recognised the message, her eyes lit up, and with hips gyrating like a washing machine on full throttle, she steered herself into the space between my outstretched arms. I circled, as she spun around in the opposing direction, eyes flashing over her shoulder at me, arms up, hands weaving tales of poetic grace in the air. I moved sideways, kilt swinging like a pendulum, and she followed as though it had been rehearsed. The crowd cheered, cameras flashed, and we finished to a roar of applause. I gave her a hug and she looked at me in amazement, "That was fantastic." And my 10-person fan club from Tiare Village performed a couple of Mexican Waves in appreciation.

Chatting to Kura after the show, I was astonished to learn that she had climbed Ben Nevis, the highest mountain in Scotland. But how on Earth did a lassie from Mitiaro, population about 180 people, a dot in the vastness of the Pacific Ocean, come to be climbing Ben Nevis? She told me she had lived in England for 11 years with her family, and had toured Scotland. This place is full of surprises, with no end of links with Scotland.

As I stood chatting to some people, another girl, Vivien, one of the loveliest lassies you could ever hope to meet, came over. We had met at various places in the previous three months. Born in Samoa, brought up in New Zealand, she too had visited Scotland. An accountant, she spent four years working in England after her graduation, and she had visited Edinburgh and Glasgow. Her eyes sparkled, her lips parted in a dazzling smile, and her long black hair flowed as she rushed across, "Hi Johnnie! Great to see you again."

(she'd been home to New Zealand over the festive period and had just got back). She gave me a hug, then looked accusingly into my eyes and said, "Well, aren't you going to wish me a Happy New Year?" The inviting smile that followed was all the encouragement I needed for a peck on the cheek and another hug.

"How long till you leave the island now?" she asked, still with her arms around me - and I was not in the slightest perturbed by it.

"Only another two weeks left," I mourned.

"Is that all? Oh, we'll miss you. And will you be playing here for the next two weeks?"

"Aye, in fact I'll be playing here on my last night. I leave on Thursday."

"Right, I'll make a point of being here to see you play again before you go." She gave me another hug. "See you next week, Johnnie."

"Aye." I sighed, wishing I was thirty years younger....

An American woman then came over and told me, "John, I really enjoyed your playing. I have never seen anything like that before, but I also wanted to tell you how magnificent you look in your kilt. It is so beautiful, and you look so... so ...oh, I am really struggling to find words." I was tempted to help her out by saying, "Handsome. Sexy?" but modesty restrained me.

"The colours are wonderful. It is so unusual to see a man wearing bright colours unless he's gay." I nearly choked on my beer. "Oh, don't get me wrong. The kilt is not in any way effeminate; it is so manly." My chest swelled an inch or two, and I affected my most manly stance. "And I was watching your body as you danced..."

Oh aye? This gets better all the time!

"You have such a natural sense of rhythm, and the way your kilt swings when you dance is just so... oh, I just think you are so *handsome!*"

Och well, you know what Californians are like. They tend to go a bit over the top - even when they are telling the truth. I thanked her for the compliment, stood back a pace, eyed her up and down, and replied, with my usual rustic, highland charm, "Aye, and you're no' bad lookin' either." She almost swooned.

"Oh John. It's such a privilege to meet you!"

She smiled at me. I smiled back at her. Then we both stopped smiling at each other and she gave me a lingering hug to formalise our acquaintance. I could hear her muffled murmurings of delight in my ear and was thinking about what the next move might be when she released me, turned to a big guy with shoulders as broad as a barn door standing behind her, and said, "John, I'd like you to meet my husband, David." Well, that brought another promising story to an anti-climactic end.

While we had been talking, a Maori woman from New Zealand had walked past and whispered in my ear how good the kilt looked. A wee while later she passed again, and now that I was free from the clutches of the American woman, she stopped this time to talk with me. "You didn't tell me your name last time," she murmured, so we exchanged names and then she too hugged me before returning to her friends.

A minute or two later, I heard another female voice squeal with delight. "Papa John!" I turned and there was an English girl I had met a few nights previously, an attractive beauty therapist who worked in one of the big hotels.

"Och, it's yersel' Mandy." I effused.

She gave me a lingering hug, "You are so sweet. You even remembered my name."

We talked for a while and she asked for my phone number. Now, don't get too carried away. I am merely a father figure, Papa

John - with the emphasis on *Papa* - a safe prospect. I may indulge in some mild flirtation, but nothing ever happens. It's fun and amuses - and amazes - the other backpackers I go out with.

Before Mandy came over to speak to me, I had been talking to a young Scottish lad. He looked in amazement at the procession of admiring ladies, shook his head, and said, "That kilt is a magnet! I'm kicking myself for not bringing mine with me."

Aye... Look and learn, laddie.

Almost as powerful an attraction as the kilt, my spoons also proved to be an object of fascination. They have brought smiles to the faces of people of every culture, and in every continent I have visited. Carved from a single piece of beech wood by a woodcarver living on the north coast of Scotland, they are shaped like tongs rather than two separate spoons, and are easy to hold.

The shafts are springy and the cupped shape of the spoons creates a hollow sound, which can be varied depending on how you strike them with the hand, ranging from a sharp clip with the edge of the hand to a mellow clop with the hand cupped over the spoon. You strike a beat with the right hand to match the rhythm of the music and let the left hand vary the sounds as it makes contact with the spoons. It is simple. Aye, the simplicity that comes from years of practice.

After Ronan and I had played at the Staircase Restaurant & Bar, an American came over to me, introduced himself as a professional drummer from Las Vegas and said, "After watching what you can do with these spoons, I am asking myself why I travel around with a complete set of drums."

That was followed by a request for me to perform at a charity concert in aid of the disabled in the Cook Islands, an event that attracted a following of my backpacker supporters from Tiare Village Hostel. As always, a feast was provided at such events, and the organisers insisted the backpackers take their share as they were delighted to see visitors to the island supporting their efforts to help the disabled. They offered them more food than they could ever eat, gave them the best seats, introduced them to their families, and invited them to join in other events coming up soon. I felt honoured to be invited to participate with so many of my Cook Island friends among the singers and musicians on a day with a high feel-good factor that affected everyone present in a positive manner.

That night I went out with a couple, a nice Kiwi guy with a charming Samoan wife, with whom I had become friends during their stay at Tiare Village. They had come to the concert "Just to see Johnnie play the spoons," had enjoyed it all, and had been impressed by the warmth and hospitality offered by the locals. They told me that seeing what I was doing here had made them think of their own future. They had their own business, and had now decided that their aim in life would be to work towards making enough money to allow them to take sufficient time off to offer voluntary help to some community in need. Never underestimate the power of example.

Dropping Ronan off at the airport for his flight to New Zealand ended another enjoyable chapter of life in the Cook Islands, and his parting words were, "I'll be back."

Driving home from the airport, I reflected on how music transcends the boundaries of language and culture, delights people of all races, and forges friendships among people of different cultures. It must be the most accessible of the arts and has that amazing power to evoke memories associated with events, people, and places. It's a delight to bring pleasure to people through performing with others, even with such a humble instrument as the spoons. These spoons travelled five times round the world with me, until on the night train from Bangkok to Chaing Mai…. but that is a story for later.

My one regret in life is that I never learned to play the bagpipes. That is what everyone expects when they see a man in a kilt.

CHAPTER 27

Daily Life

Each day on Rarotonga started with a shower at 6:30 a.m. followed by breakfast on the deck of the chalet, eating fresh pawpaw (papaya), or mangoes which grow on the trees in the grounds, followed by cereal and toast. A light lunch and a hearty meal in the evening made up my three meals per day.

A couple of resident mynah birds perched on the Tiare Village sign just outside my chalet and screeched at me every morning, demanding some food. They are cute, but cheeky, and will come right into the kitchen for something to eat if you leave the door open. I developed an affection for them, but their indiscriminate toilet habits discouraged me from inviting them in for tea.

I was working again on a voluntary basis and enjoying it. In addition to my special needs work I had managed to fit in a range of teaching experiences in sport, craft, and music. The boys, many of whom were keen traditional drummers, were attracted by my playing of the spoons: "That's really cool," and I was invited to join the percussion section of the school band for the concert at the end of term. I had also done talks based on my travels, covered for absent teachers, and after I was asked to address the whole school at an assembly, they all knew who I was.

Teaching sailing and canoeing was a pleasant way to end the week's work on Friday afternoons. The small sailing dinghies had just one sail to control, good for beginners. The canoes were traditional Polynesian outrigger canoes, vaka, in the local language. With only one paddle, you make several strokes on one side, then change hands and paddle on the other side. That week there had been an international festival of canoeing on the island with paddlers from Canada, Hawaii, Tahiti, Cook Islands, Fiji, Samoa, Australia, and New Zealand. The big six-man outriggers presented an impressive sight racing round the island, a distance of about 20 miles, powered by the muscles of those hardy men. And what muscles! These guys had biceps thicker than my thighs.

Few teachers there had the kind of experience I'd had in dealing with pupils with special needs. The education department budget was insufficient to provide the necessary on-going support and there were no training facilities for special needs teachers. One wee boy with cerebral palsy charmed me. Strapped into his wheelchair, even his head had to be supported, his face creased with delight every time I spoke to him. He could only utter strangulated squeals of pleasure, the nearest thing he could get to words, his mouth wide open and his eyes dancing with delight. Some willing helpers worked as assistants with the kids with cerebral palsy, learning as they went along, but few were prepared to meet the challenge of dealing with the severe mood swings and challenging behaviour of an autistic child. That job was given to me.

At an end of term social evening, a barbecue arranged by the school board, the principal made a touching speech thanking me for my contribution to the school. She finished by saying, "You have been a gift from God, John. It was amazing how you arrived out of the blue, just when we needed you most."

I was then presented with a gift, a pendant made of carved mother of pearl with a variety of traditional carvings and the words *Meitaki maata John* (Thank you very much John) inscribed on it. The pendant is in the shape of a traditional Polynesian fish hook, a symbol of life and a safe journey over water. Carved patterns on the face of the hook include sea birds (*manu tai*) which symbolise good news to the fisherman, indicating fish to catch, and to the sailor, an impending landfall. *Tikitiki tangata*, a pattern originating from the island of Mangaia, is symbolic of unity and strength. The wave pattern (*ngaru*) symbolises power, and the weave pattern (*raranga*) represents the warp and weft of life. All the symbols seemed appropriate to my terrestrial nomadic life-style, and my sailing when back home in Scotland.

The following day, I was in turmoil when the principal asked me to consider staying, with the offer of a full year's contract with salary. And just to pile on the agony, the mother of the autistic boy I had worked with was also in the principal's office and offered me a two-bedroom bungalow, rent-free, if I would stay and continue to work with her son. With a salary and free accommodation I could live in the Cook Islands and save most of my UK pension for a year. As on my previous visit to the Cook Islands, when the minister on Mauke asked me to stay on that small island to teach, the invitation was very tempting. I struggled with my emotions. I had enjoyed my work. The pupils were a delight, and vied at the end of the period to be allowed to express a vote of thanks to me for teaching the class, no matter what age they were. That's another aspect of the culture I like: they all wanted to make that wee speech thanking me for what I had done for them. But would I still enjoy being here if tied to a contract for a year? Or would I find it even more difficult to leave at the end of that year? The debate raged in my mind.

As with the offer of a job the previous year on Mauke, freedom swung the argument. The freedom to roam at will and visit other places had become precious to me. With many doubts in my mind, and with considerable regret, I declined the offer and remained a terrestrial tramp.

In common with many other island communities across the world, time in the Cook Islands is almost an irrelevance. Time was here before we arrived, and time will be here long after we have gone, so there is no need to rush. Punctuality is a concept that seems irrelevant in island communities. In general, islands instil a more relaxed and tolerant attitude.

This was typified by two stories in the Cook Islands News. With little serious crime, only a handful of prisoners were locked up in the state prison, so it is understandable that the prison regime might be more relaxed than in some countries. Indeed, it was so relaxed that the only prisoner in the female section, serving a life sentence for the attempted murder of her husband, had been found to be pregnant - for the second time in the five years she had been in prison! The father in both cases was a male prisoner. Well, keeping the prisoners happy is good for morale.

However, while Cook Islanders may be pretty laid back, they are not without remarkable ingenuity. A series of recent burglaries had the police perplexed. The usual suspects were already locked up in prison and no leads were found to implicate anyone else, until the burglars were caught on a surveillance camera and recognised. They were two inmates of the national prison! The enterprising pair had been breaking out at night, breaking into shops and businesses, and hiding the loot for disposal later.

Then they sneaked back into prison before the morning roll call. Brilliant! What better alibi than to be locked up in prison?

My knowledge of the island was in demand again, guiding backpackers on the trek through the jungle from coast to coast. I also taught them how to husk, crack, drink, and eat a coconut and offered some bush medicine remedies: how to soothe away the inflammation caused by mosquito bites using the juice of the aloe vera plant; which seeds to eat to cure diarrhoea, and how to get rid of intestinal worms. I called it Papa John's Jungle Survival Course.

During the hottest and most humid time of year, the jungle was green and lush with huge ferns, vines and other creepers forming dense undergrowth, and trekking through the forest was a sweaty business. The route across the island involved a steep scramble up to the volcanic pinnacle in the centre, The Needle. My two young companions on one occasion were not very fit. Peter sat on a rock gasping, "I hope I'm half as fit as you, John, when I reach your age." He wasn't even half as fit in his mid-twenties! But it gave him something to aspire to. Hassu, an Indian, had a tough time on that uphill section, clutching his chest, gasping for breath. I was becoming concerned about him, but he made it to the top… gasp… swearing that he would now… gasp… no buts or maybes… gasp… give up smoking. Aye, right! His resolve to give up smoking did last - until we reached the road on the other side of the island where he lit up again as we waited for the bus. No self discipline, these young guys!

The reward for the sweaty labour on this trek was a swim in the pool below the waterfall near the end. Descending the final slope through dense undergrowth, shirt and shorts saturated with sweat cling to your body. You strip off the shirt and leave it to dry in the sun and plunge headlong into the refreshing water of the pool, luxuriate there for a while, swim under the waterfall and feel the cold water pounding down on your scalp. It revives you so well that you feel you could walk all the way back over the mountain instead of taking the bus back home - at least, that's how I felt.

Waterfall

However, my young friends had no intention of becoming involved in such madness. They were relieved to have survived what they regarded as a challenging expedition and preferred to walk the last mile to the road to wait for the bus.

A group of people we had met in the jungle had skipped the swim at the waterfall and were already at the roadside, eating sandwiches and drinking fruit drinks brought by two cars that were waiting for them. They immediately offered to share their food and drink, insisting that it was the least they could do, as I had steered them on to the right track after they had been about to wander off the route in the wrong direction. It is not unusual for people to get lost on this trek. Some have had to spend the night in the jungle before being found by a search party next day.

The irony is that it took a Scotsman, from half way round the world, to guide them across their native island. They were all Cook Islanders, now living in New Zealand.

The week before Christmas was dominated by preparations for the hostel Christmas dinner. It was agreed that we would all make a contribution towards the cost of food and Adrienne, the manager, allowed us the use of the hostel minibus to bring the food from the shops, on the condition that I was to be the driver. Perhaps my seniority hinted that I might be a more responsible driver than some of the younger people. There also seemed to be a unanimous assumption among the backpackers that I would direct operations: organise the catering, delegate tasks to a workforce of backpackers who were willing to help prepare the food, but needed some direction.

The dinner was planned for the evening to allow plenty of time for preparation. I had been invited to a christening in the morning, with lunch to follow with some Cook Island friends. Bob Hunter, a local fishing boat owner and game fisherman, had asked me to attend his first-born son's christening. Bob, half-Irish, half-Cook Islander, is a big, handsome guy about six feet five inches tall with a physique to match. His wife, Avera, works with her parents and sister in the family business, the Staircase Restaurant, where the weekly island night shows are held, and I got free meals for bringing so much trade to them for the Island Night Shows. That family are among my oldest Cook Island friends.

I knew several of Bob's family too: he's one of eight siblings. He approached me one day and told me he would feel honoured if I would attend the christening. "We would really like you to be there with us John. Everyone in the family thinks the world of you and I respect you so much, not just for what you do here, but for the kind of guy you are." I was touched by such a tribute and accepted the invitation.

The baby was christened at the start of the Christmas day church service at Ngatangia, on the other side of the island. After a few of the usual formalities, the minister dispensed with the sermon and the usual order of service. Instead, he invited the members of his congregation from the three villages in the parish, and the visitors, to form four teams for a singing competition.

The village choirs each had to sing a traditional Maori hymn, with the usual separate male and female parts; the visitors were allocated the much easier carol, Silent Night. It had become a light-hearted affair now, the residents of each village singing their hearts out, trying to better each other. The visitors were never in the running for the top spot against such intense and skilled competition.

The winners were decided by how much money was offered as a mark of appreciation for each choir's efforts, three separate bowls being placed at the front of the church, one for each village. When the singing was over we all placed our offerings in the bowl of the village whose choir we thought the best. It was all good-natured fun and probably resulted in a much better collection than any conventional offering would have raised – and the singing was fantastic, loud, passionate, with some exquisite harmonies.

At times, the male line consisted of a series of grunts, "oo-ah-ay-yoo-ah," underscoring the melodic female line. It sounds primitive, but it blended so well. Their enjoyment of their art is clear: they sing, and they swing with it, heads and bodies swaying to the rhythm. The village choirs rehearse in the village meeting places, usually open-air, in the evenings before Christmas and the sound of the hymns drifts across the village in the still evening air, as the sun sets behind the palm trees. It is one of the characteristic sounds of the Cook Islands.

After such a fun service, everyone left the church in good spirits. The christening party went to Mann and Sissi's house, Avera's parents, where lunch was served. The baby's godfather was another friend of mine, Sonny, the masterful lead ukelele player in the string band that had adopted me as their 'guest star' spoons player for the Wednesday night performances at the Whatever Bar. My companion at lunch was Sir Apenera Short, Mann's father, the former queen's representative for the Cook Islands. I had been deeply saddened by the news of his wife's death a few weeks earlier. Lady Maui had been a real sweetie, a true Lady. It was such a homely gathering and I felt very much among friends.

By 3 p.m. I was back at the hostel helping to peel potatoes and directing the efforts of everyone involved in preparing the Christmas dinner. It all came together successfully, and everyone agreed that a traditional Christmas dinner, but with chicken instead of turkey which is very expensive here, with wine, for only NZ$10 (about £4 in UK money) was good value. After dinner, most of us sat up late, talking, to complete what had been a very sociable day.

I then had to pack my rucksack and be up at 6 a.m. for my morning flight to Mangaia, an island where I hoped to escape the pressures of the busy life I had been leading on Rarotonga, to spend a week relaxing, reading, writing, and exploring at my leisure.

That was what I thought I'd be doing on Rarotonga, but somehow things never quite work out that way. It's interesting how a place and its people can develop expectations of you, and pressures develop over time. Or is it my nature that's the problem: if life becomes too relaxed, I have to stir things up a bit and create pressure for myself?

CHAPTER 28

Mangaia

The small 12-seater Bandierante aircraft took off from Rarotonga in bright sunshine, but 180 miles to the southeast, Mangaia lay obscured behind an ominous wall of slate-grey cloud, streaked by flashes of lightning. Mutterings of disquiet rippled among the passengers. In these wee planes, you can look over the shoulder of the pilot and see what's ahead. The pilot skirted around the thunder clouds, missing the worst of the storm, but we bounced about in its peripheral turbulence. We approached Mangaia fast in the turbulent air, bounced hard on the crushed coral airstrip, and taxied to the terminal, a grand title for what was a roof supported at each end by a wall. It was similar to those on Mauke, Mitiaro, Atiu, and Aitutaki, all of which have airstrips on the northeast corner of the island with the sea on one side, the palms and the bush on the other, with a dirt road running parallel to the runway. As always on the islands, a crowd waited to meet relatives off the plane, or were simply curious to see who was arriving.

I strolled over to the terminal and was greeted with "Welcome to Mangaia," by a smiling girl who was waiting to greet someone else. "Hey, you're from Scotland!" exclaimed the young man with her, his eyes wide as he took in the elements of my attire: kilt, sporran, belt, socks and brogues. It was clear that I was a visitor - maybe it was the brogues that gave me away for the locals all wore flip-flops (translated: jandals, or thongs, to Kiwis and Aussies).

More people spoke to me as I waited to get my rucksack from the trailer - no baggage carousel here - satisfying their curiosity, as is the way of the islands. So far, no one seemed to know me, but it only took a couple of days to change that with calls of "John!" and friendly waves as I drove around the island on my hired motorbike.

Next day, one of the neighbours introduced me to another of the island foods I hadn't tried before. Ti, pronounced 'tee', was a survival food in the old days in times of famine. The roots of the cordyline plant are placed in an umu (earth oven) and cooked for about three days. The roots are long, fibrous, and as thick as a man's forearm. After cooking, they are sliced into small pieces and chewed along with pieces of coconut. Although the root fibres are indigestible and you have to spit them out after chewing, the juice from them tastes like treacle, and it goes so well with the coconut. I suppose the heat of the umu converts the sugar stored in the roots into treacle, or molasses. They harvest the roots only every few years as a village cultural activity to let the children know how their ancestors survived. I had thought it would serve as a sweet after dinner, but the juice feels pretty corrosive on the tooth enamel. My neighbour had other uses for the roots: cut up and placed in boiling water, the extract is released and the resulting liquor is strained and left, with some yeast added to it, to ferment for a few days to make bush beer.

Mangaia, like Mitiaro, Muake and Atiu is a raised coral island. Formerly an atoll, about 23 million years ago it was forced upwards, bringing the coral reef out of the sea. The reef then fossilised to form a hard, sharp collar of rock called makatea, which encircles the island, up to thirty metres high in places. Enclosed within the ring of makatea, the reddish ash of the volcanic cone has been enriched by the composted fallen leaves of trees and plants to create a superb soil for planting. Light and friable with a high iron content, it is ideal for growing pineapples, claimed to be the sweetest to be found anywhere, and other fruits and vegetables. The makatea is free draining and is riddled with limestone caves.

I visited some of these with a guide, Tuara, who had a fund of stories about the past and some of the strange people who lived in the caves. The bones of The Tongan, one of these characters, can be seen where he died. No one knows when he died, but it is thought it must have been at least two or three centuries ago. Inside the cave, this clever man made a wee stellar map resembling a rock garden in which the stones marked the positions of the most prominent stars. It is very accurate and can be used as a compass, its four corners aligning perfectly with north, south, east and west. Some of the caves were used as burial chambers, and in others people hid to escape human sacrifice. When tribes warred with one another, the victors always sacrificed some of their prisoners to the gods as an act of thanksgiving. The caves offered a way of evading capture. Not many people were happy about going in there in the days before electric torches, and with only flickering fire torches the stalactites and stalagmites must have looked even more mysterious. The entrances were small and easily defended, and the labyrinth of tunnels inside also made it easy to defend against intruders.

When one entire tribe hid in a such a cave, the opposition tried to starve them out, but failed. They wondered how they managed to survive for so long without food. Water was plentiful in the caves, but what did they find to eat? Simple. Resorting to cannibalism, they made their own sacrifices from among the tribe and survived for several weeks underground. The bones of those who drew the short straw and ensured the survival of the rest are still there. It is fascinating place.

With the makatea up to 30 metres (100 feet) high and precipitous on the inland side, the scenery is quite grand in places as the old reef wall, once festooned with marine growth, pearl clams, patrolled by sharks and home to countless fish, is now festooned with ferns and creepers. The interior, which was once a deep lagoon, is now a fertile valley patterned with taro beds and fruit plantations and dotted with small lakes.

The original villages, small communities of kikau huts made from timber posts and woven pandanus leaves, used to be sited here close to the plantations. Tuara was born in one of the last of these traditional huts in 1958, but now all the people live in three villages on smoothed off areas of the makatea. That's where the churches were built, such substantial buildings requiring a rock base for their foundations. The people now live in simple concrete dwellings with corrugated iron roofs. The old kikau houses rotted away in a few years, leaving no trace of their existence; by contrast, several of the concrete houses, which have been abandoned as the population has declined, will lie as roofless ruins for centuries, if they are not demolished. There are several in that state, signifying the main problem faced by many island communities: how to keep themselves economically viable and sustain their populations. The hills in the interior, former volcanic ash cones, rise from these fertile valleys. Rainforests with dense undergrowth cover the low ground and the higher slopes have been planted with several species of conifer to protect the soft ground against erosion. It is heartening to see such awareness of conservation here, with numerous notices reminding visitors, and locals, about the sensitive nature of the environment.

With the makatea rising out of the sea, there are no beaches worth mentioning on the island, nor is there a lagoon with a protective reef. A coral shelf extends a short distance from the shore and drops to the ocean floor, about 14,000 feet below. The only place to swim is in the tiny harbour, little more than a landing stage, where a passage has been blasted through the coral shelf to allow a barge to transfer cargo from ship to shore. Severely damaged - ripped apart is a fair description - by recent cyclones, the jetty would have been closed off for safety reasons in any litigious western country, but here they carry on using it. Their survival depends upon it.

The harbour also serves as the island's swimming pool, where youngsters throw themselves off the fragmented jetty into the powerful surge that roars in from the ocean. It also serves as a haven for a few vakas, the traditional outrigger fishing canoes. While the type of craft is traditional, the method of propulsion is modern; instead of paddling they now have Yamaha outboard engines fastened to brackets fitted between the canoe and the outrigger. Apart from that innovation, fishing goes on as it has done for generations; a bamboo rod and line on the reef, a net to cast in the water, or skin diving and spear-fishing. This is sustainable fishing; effective without plundering the sea or damaging the marine environment, and without any commercial pressure as the catch is only for local consumption. Boats are inexpensive. Cut down a tree, hollow out the trunk and tie on a branch to serve as an outrigger for stability. The engine, if fitted, is the only expense. Labour is free. There is plenty of time on the island for such a project.

The weather was changeable during my stay; hot and humid with thunder and torrential showers, or blustery with severe squalls. I got caught in a downpour once on the motorbike, in a steep valley among the hills. I had a waterproof jacket with me so I managed to get my camera bag covered, but the roads were dirt tracks. I had dropped down a steep hill before the rains came, and had to climb another steep slope to get out, but the rain had turned the surface of the track into a greasy, red clay. On the valley bottom, I was sloshing and sliding through large, red-coloured puddles, but on the steep slope driving was impossible. The wheels of the bike slithered sideways and spun in the muddy ruts. I had to get off, keep the engine in gear using minimum throttle, and push the bike, but my sandals had no grip in the sticky red clay. I slipped and went down in the mud with the bike beside me. Mud wrestling with a motorbike isn't much fun: I was covered in mud from head to foot. It also choked up the gap between the wheels and the mudguards. Several times I had to claw out a red clay plug with my hands before I could move the bike forward and the sliding and spinning rear wheel sprayed me with mud. I was a rich terracotta colour by the time I got back. Standing still, I could have been mistaken for a garden gnome.

I had planned to make an entry to the social scene on Mangaia on Boxing Day as there was to be a dance in the village that night, but the grand-mother of the owner of the place I was staying at died that afternoon. Aged 89, she was known to everyone, and was probably related to everyone too, so that night the mamas were busy preparing a feast for the hundreds of mourners who would be at the funeral next day, many of whom came over in chartered flights from Rarotonga. The family were busy preparing the body for the funeral. There were no professional undertakers. They don't waste any time: in the tropical heat a body decomposes fast, so you die one day and get buried the next. It also showed how Air Rarotonga accepts its obligation to provide a social service to the islands. On such occasions, the pilots always take on extra flying duties to allow mourning relatives to get to the islands on chartered flights. That knocked out the dance on Boxing Day evening.

At Christmas and New Year many exiles return to their place of birth to visit relatives, flying in from Australia, New Zealand, Rarotonga, or the other Cook Islands. Most people engage in family activities with relatives. On the Friday night, the place livened up with a dance, featuring a popular band brought over from Rarotonga. As soon as I entered, I was called over by Tua, a young man about 18 years old, sitting with some boys and girls, all of whom I had met at the harbour. A chair was pulled out for me, I was welcomed like an old friend, and was introduced to parents, aunties, uncles, and cousins. Everybody is related to one another here, and to several of the people I knew on Rarotonga.

It reminded me of the village hall dances in the Highlands of Scotland with people of all ages attending, mingling, regardless of age. An interesting feature during an interlude was a string band contest, several local bands featuring ukuleles, guitars, and the odd base drum vying for the honours. This was interspersed with displays of traditional dancing by a girl in her late teens, and another, about six years old, who demonstrated a skill and poise beyond her years.

With the temperamental weather restricting my plans for further exploration of the island, I spent the time reading three books, writing, and sleeping. And thinking. Why am I drawn to quiet backwaters like this? So many people would find it boring with 'nothing to do,' but that depends on your outlook. If you've nothing to do, it is your own fault. Some people come from Europe and can't bear to leave the place - they usually marry a local girl. I couldn't imagine that happening to me at my age. Yet I couldn't believe how quickly the time passed and how varied and full the days seemed. Again, I wondered how it would feel to stay longer and become more involved in the life of such a remote community.

If I were to come again, should I spend most of my time on one of the outer islands rather than on Rarotonga? Living and working in such a society had a certain appeal, yet I felt rooted to life on Rarotonga. I had made so many friends there. It offered a nice half-way house between modern and ancient ways of life. It had insinuated itself into my consciousness as my second home. I would soon be back on Raro, but for only two more weeks before I started travelling again. No matter where I travel there is always a restless urge to find out what is round the next bend in the road, over the next hill, beyond the distant horizon - the torment of the terrestrial tramp. But it keeps life interesting.

CHAPTER 29

Romantic Drama

While driving around Rarotonga one Sunday afternoon on my motorbike, a name seemed to thrust itself at me from a roadside gravestone - Duncan Munro. The grave was not in a cemetery, but that is not unusual. Internment on family land is normal here. Land cannot be bought or sold and, in a culture in which ancestors are revered, it means the descendants are always on hand to care for the graves. That such a Scottish name should appear on a grave in the heart of a Polynesian island intrigued me. I stopped and read the inscription:

In Loving Memory

Of

Our Dear Dad

628048 Pte. DUNCAN MUNRO

47th Bat. Canadian Expeditionary Force

Beloved Husband of Teina J Tuka

Born Scotland 12/8/1880

Died Rarotonga 11/6/1954

I had an overwhelming feeling that Duncan Munro may have had connections with Easter Ross, the heartland of Clan Munro, a part of Scotland in which I had lived for several years before

I retired. I also felt that, behind the words on that headstone, there might be a story worth telling. I wanted to find some of his descendants to find out more.

Do you believe in coincidence? Well, a week or two later, after playing spoons with the band at the Whatever Bar, I was invited over to a group of patrons who had expressed an interest in seeing the spoons and talking about the kilt. They introduced themselves.

"I am so pleased to see you wearing your kilt," Anna Rasmussen told me. "My grandfather came from Scotland."

"Oh, what was his name?"

"Duncan Munro."

" What! Duncan Munro whose grave is on the back road at Arorangi?"

"Yes, that's right. You've seen the grave then?"

"Aye! And I am intrigued by it. I have been trying to find some of his descendants to learn more about him. I lived in the heart of Clan Munro territory for years. Can you tell me where in Scotland he was born?"

"I can't remember the name of the village, but I can give it to you if you come to my house tomorrow afternoon. I have some information about him there."

That gave me a great start. Anna had a heap of information, including her grandmother's family tree that went back about 800 years to the first Polynesian settlers who came to Rarotonga. She also gave me more contacts, other relatives who had information they might be willing to share. I did some further research in the Cook Islands before I left, and on my return to Scotland, searched both the Scottish and Canadian records and contacted some other descendants. There was indeed a story behind the information on that gravestone: a tale of adventure, drama and romance.

In 1916, lying in a military hospital in France, his body ripped apart by shellfire, this son of a humble Scottish shepherd could never in his wildest dreams have imagined that one day he would marry into a royal family on the other side of the world, in a place he had probably never heard of - Rarotonga.

Born on 12 August 1880 at Achmelvich, a tiny community on the rugged northwest coast of Scotland, Duncan was the eldest of the thirteen children of Donald Munro and Margaret MacLeod, who later moved to Dornoch in the county of Sutherland. His grandfather, John Munro, had been born at Culcraggie, Alness, in 1818, a mere stone's throw from where I had lived, and his great-grandfather Donald, son of Andrew, was born at Glen Glass in 1789, both right in the heart of Munro country, so my hunch had been right.

Around the end of the 19th century, like many of his countrymen, Duncan reckoned that Canada might offer a more prosperous future and responded to a call for lumberjacks to harvest the vast forests of British Columbia. It was not an easy life in the Canadian logging camps. Felling huge trees with axe and crosscut saw was strenuous work. Usually in remote country, the territory of the grizzly bear, black bear, cougar and wolf, the camps offered little in the way of home comforts; a roof over your head, a deal board to sleep on, and primitive cooking facilities. However, there was no shortage of work and it paid well. As a result of letters home, some of his brothers joined him in the early 1900s. This was male-only territory and it is little wonder that Duncan was still a bachelor in his mid-thirties.

But in 1914, in far off Sarajevo, a single assassin's bullet changed the course of world history - and Duncan's future - when

Archduke Ferdinand of Austria was struck down. Within a few weeks Europe, and much of the rest of the world, was plunged into war. With such a horrific casualty rate in the trenches of France and Flanders, reinforcements were required to support and relieve the regular battalions, and across the countries of the British Commonwealth men rallied to the call to arms. On 12th June 1915, at Vernon, British Columbia, Duncan enlisted in the 47th (British Columbia) Battalion, Canadian Expeditionary Force. It was a 'hostilities only' battalion, a unit that existed only for the duration of the war, after which it would be disbanded and its men would return to civilian life, if they survived.

After initial training at the Royal Westminster Regiment headquarters near Vancouver, the 47th battalion sailed from Montreal on 13th November 1915 on the Canadian Pacific liner *Missanabie*. Nine days later, the ship docked at Plymouth, England. Several months of further military training followed in England, until 10th August 1916, when the 47th were shipped across the English Channel to Le Havre, and transported to the trenches to join the Canadian 4th Division. Arriving at the front, they were plunged into the thick of the action in the horrific and bloody Battle of the Somme.

On 11th November 1916, after months of deadlock, the 47th were dug in at Regina Trench when the order came to attack enemy lines. Going over the top, they were greeted by the clatter of enemy machine-gun fire and the boom of exploding mortars. Advancing into that deadly hail of fire with bayonets fixed, men fell, screaming, wounded, or dying. Despite the carnage, the attack was successful and the deadlock was broken at last. But fate was yet to strike a cruel blow.

Duncan's war record reveals that he was struck by a fragment of shrapnel during this engagement. However, his eldest daughter in New Zealand gave a more graphic account of the events that were to change her father's life. Duncan was detailed to escort a group of German prisoners back to his own lines but, in the confusion of battle, seeing a group of Germans coming towards the Canadian lines, his own comrades opened fire. A mortar shell exploded behind him and a piece of shrapnel ripped through his lower back, took part of one of his lower vertebrae away, lacerated his bowel in several places, and passed right through the front of his abdomen. Duncan fell, bleeding, into the mud.

With blood pouring from his body, his German prisoners came to his aid. They helped him to his feet and supported him back to the safety of his trench where they surrendered themselves.

Duncan's war now became a personal one, a battle against debilitating injuries. After first aid in the field he was transferred a couple of days later to the military hospital at Camiers, on the coast near Boulogne. Following surgery there, he was shipped back to England, where he required further surgery and treatment for almost a year at hospitals in Norfolk, Hastings, Shoreham, and The Duchess of Connaught Hospital at Taplow, Berkshire. After a short spell of leave to visit his widowed mother in Scotland, he was sent to Liverpool to embark on the *Llandovery Castle* on 19th September 1917. On his return to Canada, he had a further spell of hospital treatment in Victoria BC, and was discharged from military service on 6th July 1918.

As a token of gratitude for his war service, the Canadian government granted him ten acres of undeveloped land on Vancouver Island, but his land was mostly a shallow lake. Undaunted, he and his brother Findlay set about draining the lake and turned the land into a productive farm they called Summerland, but the demanding physical work and the damp climate of Vancouver Island did not suit Duncan's war wounds. He transferred the title to his land to his brother Findlay for a nominal fee of $1, and set sail for New Zealand to take up employment with the New Zealand Government. In 1919 Duncan was deployed to the Cook Islands, recording and shipping the copra harvest.

Duncan was then 39 years old and still unattached, but not for long. Soon after he arrived on Rarotonga, he caught the attention of 17 year-old Teina Tuka, and it is fairly certain that Teina's tall, striking figure also caught Duncan's eye. This was no ordinary girl. Teina, the short form of her full name, Teinangaro Ki Raro Te Moana Matake'u Tuka, was a princess of the royal line, Te Ariki Marokura Arera Tuarea, a line of Arikis, or kings, who could trace their ancestry back 800 years to the famed Tangi'ia Nui, who around the year 1200, migrated across the Pacific from Raiatea, an island near Tahiti, and settled with his tribe on Rarotonga. Genealogy is important in Polynesian culture, and Teina's family tree had been memorised and passed down with each succeeding generation in a fashion similar to the Celtic oral traditions of Scotland.

It is not known when or how they met, but that there was a mutual attraction seems to be without doubt. However, Teina's association with Duncan caused her parents much consternation, for she had already been betrothed to a suitable young Cook islander of similar importance; a prospective marriage not only of two people, but of their inherited lands. Land is wealth in Polynesian society and the joining of two young people, each with considerable lands, would bring more wealth and power to both families.

But Teina was a spirited lass, with a mind of her own. In open defiance of her parent's wishes, she eloped with Duncan on a vessel sailing to the small island of Manuae when he went to collect the copra harvest. Their first-born child, Peggy, was conceived during this voyage. In any family, such an act may have caused a furore, but Teina wasn't just from any family. She was from a royal family, and her impetuous act in running off with Duncan had destroyed all prospects of a profitable marriage to her arranged suitor. That would not have enamoured her to anyone in either family. Furthermore, one set of grandparents had been missionaries to the outer islands at a time when the missionaries were trying to discourage cohabitation in favour of a formal Christian marriage, so her elopement would not have gone down well with them either.

Teina, now aged 18, gave birth to their daughter, Peggy, on 11th September 1920. As is not uncommon in Polynesian society, the child of the young mother was cared for by Duncan and Teina's very close friends, Mr and Mrs Hopkins, who looked after Peggy while Duncan and Teina continued to travel together to pursue his work among the outer islands. However, Mr & Mrs Hopkins could not bear to part with Peggy when they returned and she grew up with them, but always in close proximity to her real family. It wasn't until she was 14 years old that Peggy learned that her neighbours, Papa and Mama Munro, were her natural parents and their younger children, with whom she played, were her brothers and sisters.

This may seem strange to the western mind, but the concept of the extended family is very strong in Polynesian culture. In cases like this, the notion of *family* can extend beyond blood relations. Older people are respected for their wisdom and knowledge, children are loved regardless of who gave birth to them, and there is evidence that such domestic arrangements are capable of bringing considerable enrichment to young lives, and a sense of belonging to an extended family community.

The strength of Duncan and Teina's love for each other enabled their relationship to survive the ructions caused by their elopement. After three more children had arrived, they formalised their relationship with a civil marriage at the registry office at Avarua, Rarotonga, on 6th December 1926. They had 10 children altogether, one of whom, Findlay, was stillborn.

At the time of his marriage, Duncan's occupation was given as trader. Teina sold the fruit and vegetables, the water-melons, paw paws, mangoes, breadfruit, and taro grown on their land in the valley behind the village of Arorangi. He also developed a citrus plantation, growing lemons, limes and oranges. Around 1935, he built a shop and traded at Tukavaine, behind Avarua, the main settlement on Rarotonga. The dramas were now over and Duncan and Teina lived the rest of their lives in conventional matrimony, working together to support their large family. Their children and grandchildren grew up, and some migrated to New Zealand in search of a more prosperous life, just as Duncan had done half a century before, when he left Scotland for Canada.

Duncan died of heart failure in 1954, aged 78. Teina contracted elephantiasis from a mosquito bite and died three years later, aged 54. She was buried beside her beloved Scottish husband on the family land at Arorangi.

Today, the descendants of the Scottish shepherd's son and the Cook Island princess are spread across the Cook Islands, New Zealand, Australia, Samoa, and Europe. Intensely proud of their Scottish ancestry, they held a family gathering in December 2004 in Auckland. With over 100 descendants, the South Pacific branch of the Clan Munro is in robust health.

CHAPTER 30

Cyclone

Maybe it was nature's grand plan to get me acclimatised to Scottish weather, for Rarotonga had just experienced some of its wettest weather on record as a cyclone barrelled its way across the South Pacific. Reports were coming in of severe damage in Samoa, Fiji, and New Caledonia, and Rarotonga was now in its path. One section of the coast road had to be closed as the waves were pouring over the sea wall, and boat owners were advised to lift their boats out of the harbour.

The roads were littered with debris: broken branches of trees, palm fronds, coconuts, flood debris, and the occasional fallen tree. Before the storm reached its peak, I had gone to buy some fish for dinner, but on the way back a vicious squall buffeted me with such fury, with the rain coming down in sheets, stinging my face. A motorbike wasn't the best thing to be on in such conditions. It was impossible to see ahead. I pulled in towards the harbour, jumped off the bike and took shelter by the Police Maritime Surveillance centre where there was some cover, and moments later a tree crashed down across the road I would have been travelling on. After the squall passed, I took to the road once more and negotiated my way past the fallen tree. Maybe someone 'up there' was looking after me.

All night long the wind blasted the island and the rain thundered down. The following day, everything became very still in the early afternoon. Then the thunder rolled and the rain came down harder than ever before. It was like living underneath a waterfall. Which was just what some kids across the road were enjoying, standing under the waterfall of rain that ran off the roof of their house, squealing with delight. After the heavens had emptied it became still and quiet, but only for a short time before the wind started screaming and tearing at the palm fronds once more, trees lashed their boughs in fury, and the rain came down like bullets again. Roads had now become muddy rivers, drainage ditches were unable to cope with the volume of water pouring off the mountains, and the force of the water ate away at road surfaces leaving deep potholes, unseen in the muddy waters that covered them.

I can't resist a good storm, and as the wind began to abate later that afternoon, I ventured out to have a look at the sea. The harbour entrance was lost in a grey mist as the wind whipped spindrift off the wave tops and blew it across the basin like smoke. The wharf was awash. A few fishing boats and the rusting, island trader, Miss Mataroa, danced on a demented sea, bouncing against the edge of the wharf, knocking fragments of concrete off it, to the accompaniment of the sonorous clanging of their hulls. I wondered how much more punishment they could take before they would spring a leak and sink. They did survive, albeit with a few dents, and the loss of a lot of paintwork.

At the old harbour, which is much smaller, the sea had wrecked Trader Jack's Restaurant and was tearing off the roof of an adjacent building, then swept across the road and underneath the new court room which had been been built on stilts. The steps up to the doorway provided a good vantage point to observe the mayhem at the old harbour, and in the midst of it all, youngsters with small surf boards where having a whale of a time. They surfed in through the harbour, over the wharf, and across the main road. It looked suicidal, but I admired their courage and skill.

Trader Jack's

At Arorangi, the beach was littered with upturned picnic tables, uprooted trees, and broken coral. Huge seas piled upon the reef which acted as a barrier to the full force of the waves. I parked the bike by the road and walked to the beach as the tide was falling. I know from my years of experience of sailing that rogue waves can occur randomly, and just such a wave surged over the reef as I reached the beach. It rose much higher than the rest, broke over the reef, and a maelstrom of frothing water raged over the lagoon. I turned and ran for the trees. The tsunami raced up the beach and through the trees. I grasped the trunk of a palm. The sea lifted me off my feet and whipped off my flip-flops, lumps of broken coral tore at my legs as I clung to the tree, waist deep in water. The surge continued over the road, swirling round the motorbike, before receding. I was relived it did not take the bike with it. Soaked from the waist down, legs scarred and bleeding by the lumps of coral that were swept around them, I wasted no more time sightseeing. The flip-flops had been swept into the sea, so there was no point in looking for them. I jumped on the bike, barefoot, and headed for home.

Effect of cyclone

Over a period of four days it had been reported that 212 mm (about 9inches) of rain fell. The Saturday alone recorded 94mm (about 4 inches) in one day. Even by Scottish standards, that was wet weather. Despite the torrential rain, only a few low-lying homes were flooded. The landscape here is kind: the water runs easily off the steep mountains and into the sea.

There's not much you can do in such weather, but it does teach you to be patient and philosophical. It had been a period of enforced rest, like a week-long Scottish Sabbath: a time to read, to think, to reflect on events. And when the weather improved, I went diving.

At 18 metres depth, the sea bed was pure white sand, the water crystal clear. I was at the bottom of a canyon on the south coast of Rarotonga, motionless, watching a sleek, reef shark glide towards me.

Its cold, unblinking eyes stared, as it swept past me. It swung round in a long curve, its tail swinging from side to side, driving it forward. It circled once more. It had surveyed its prey. It was time to attack.

It came in like a torpedo, tilted to one side, and its jaws opened, and struck with savage ferocity. That cracking noise was the sound of bone cracking. In a terrier-like frenzy, it tore the flesh away as it shook a large tuna head from side to side.

Unknown to me, our divemaster had brought a big tuna head, concealed in a sack out on the boat with him. "OK John? Ready? I'll see you on the bottom then. Off you go."

I had flicked over backwards into the sea. As I was on my way down, he tossed the fish head overboard behind me. It fell and lay on the sand a few metres from where I waited on the bottom. Within seconds the shark had appeared. That provided an interesting start to the dive.

The exceptional visibility, the canyons and gullies, tunnels and caves on that coast offer interest for the diver, for these are the resting places of the sharks that prowl each night along the reef.

Entering a long convoluted tunnel, with smaller side caves, we worked our way through with torches to a larger chamber illuminated by the pale blue light near the end of the tunnel. It was alive with sharks, resting after their night-time hunting.

Hidden by some large rocks on the floor of the cave, we stopped to observe. I counted seven sharks about two metres long. We revealed ourselves and they disappeared out of sight in a swirl of bodies and tails.

The SS Maitai, a steamship that foundered on the reef in a cyclone on Christmas Eve 1916, is now well broken up, lying in 10 metres of water. At that shallow depth we had to contend with a strong surge and swung to and fro as though suspended on a pendulum as the big pacific swells swept in and out again. The danger in such conditions is that you may be flung against a sharp piece of wreckage, so it is a good exercise in maintaining control.

What was left of the ship had become consolidated into the reef, with a century of coral growth effectively cementing it in place. The steering mechanism, the boilers, pistons, and crank shafts were all there to be seen. The hold contained bottles and old car tyres with brilliant white walls, a fashion popular at the time. Something in the composition of these tyres was an effective antifouling agent, for there was next to nothing growing on them, unlike the rest of the ship which was covered in marine growths. The tyres were for a 1916 Model T Ford, two of which had been on the ship when it was wrecked, but there is no trace of them left.

Exploration of a wreck has a special poignancy. A ship is built by craftsmen who took great pride in their work. It is more than just a vehicle for the transportation of goods; it had been a home to many, albeit for relatively short periods of time. It would have had individual handling characteristics, setting it apart from other ships, even of the same type, and it would have been, in the eyes of many, a thing of beauty, referred to as 'she,' and no doubt loved by some. This ship had died a tragic death, smashed to bits on the reef, but is still there to remind us not only of the transient nature of things, but of how even death can be a transformation that brings about life and beauty in another form. It now provides an environment where corals can flourish, and its dark passages and holds have become a sanctuary, where small fish can secrete themselves away from large predators. That wreck, like the circumstances that created it, reminded me of the Polynesian saying: if it happens, it must be for a purpose.

Time, even Island Time, that elastic, imprecise, un-pressurised concept so characteristic of life in the Cook Islands, was at last running out. The countdown towards take-off had begun for the flight to Auckland, the long haul to Hong Kong, and a shorter flight to Manila for some diving in the Philippines.

I felt a deep sadness on leaving so many friends behind, both within the backpacker community, and among the Cook Islanders. Mandy, the young beauty therapist who always greeted me with such warmth, wanted to keep in touch. "You have so much wisdom and experience to share, John. You are so easy to talk with," she told me. She had faced the dilemma of having several ardent suitors seeking her attention and needed a 'friendly uncle' to confide in, a role I seemed to be playing more often.

The final week had been full of social activity: farewell lunches and dinners with Cook Island friends and backpackers, marked by affection and hopes expressed that I would return.

Before I left, I decided to get a haircut and was ushered to a chair by Anita, a girl from the Philippines. Filipinos pop up everywhere, working abroad in service jobs: crewing on ships, housekeeping in hotels, nursing. I had met this girl a few weeks before on a night out when her boss, whom I knew, told me Anita would like to dance. I responded to the hint and had danced with her. I had seen her a couple of times since then in passing, and she always smiled and waved.

She combed my hair.

"You have nice hair colour," she said.

"Well, I can't claim any credit for that, it's all down to nature - and old age."

"You don't colour it?"

"Och no! Men don't go in for that kind of thing where I come from."

She looked into the mirror and caught my eyes.

"Do you have a family?

"Two sons."

"Where are they?"

"In Scotland."

"And your wife, is she in Scotland?" I explained my widower status.

"Have you re-married?"

"No."

"You have a girl-friend?"

"No."

"Why not?"

"I'm too old now."

"No. You are never too old. Age is just a number." I recalled the Filipino chief steward on the ship to Antarctica had said the same thing.

When she finished, she took my head in both hands, raised it and looked into the eyes of my image in the mirror. She smiled. "You look ten years younger."

"If you can work miracles like that, make it twenty," I countered. If this lassie kept talking like that, there was a risk I might lose control and find myself ordering a shave as well.

She brushed me down, looked over her handiwork and smiled at me again. "Very handsome. You'll have no trouble in finding a girl-friend now."

I smiled at her, even though I was parting with my money at this stage. It gave me some expectation about what might be in store for me when I moved on to her homeland, the Philippines.

CHAPTER 31

The Philippines

Having nothing planned in advance, I spent two days in Manila finding out where to go, arranging flights, diving, and accommodation. With over 7000 islands, there are plenty of ferries. However, these are often geriatric vessels, poorly maintained, often overloaded, and have an undesirable habit of going to the bottom of the sea. The statistics for ferry disasters in the Philippines make sombre reading, although in recent years they have tightened up on regulations. Flying is a better option, with most islands only an hour or two from Manila. With Philippine Airlines, Cebu Pacific, and Air Asia in competition on many routes, cheap flights can be obtained, if you book early. Flying at around 28,000 feet offers a perspective on life in the Philippines, revealing the remoteness of many communities, the extensive agriculture on the plains, the mountainous terrain covered in dense jungle, the paucity of roads on many islands, and the scars created by earthquakes, landslides, and volcanic eruptions.

The Philippines is an intoxicating mixture of beauty and chaos. The beauty is in the landscape, the beaches, the submarine world, and in the people: not just physical beauty, but often an inner beauty that shines through in their smiles, despite the fact that so many live in extreme poverty. It is a country of contrasts: long hours of hard work for very little pay for some, widespread idleness among others; elegant living for the few, eternal squalor for many; remarkable adaptability contrasting with deep-rooted intransigence. It is a country you can love one moment, and hate the next. It has a peculiar magnetism.

The chaos is evident in the traffic. Road signs? My first taxi driver ignored a Give Way sign at an intersection, drove into the crossing traffic, and somehow carved out a channel to allow us through. Everyone else was doing the same. It was like fairground dodgem cars, but for real. My reaction to the blatant disregard for road signs elicited a reassuring response from the driver.

"Filipinos are very good drivers. We don't need road signs. They're only for the foreigners."

Anarchy rules on the roads here. If you obey the road signs, or hesitate, you are likely to cause an accident for it will be such a surprise to the guy following you that he is likely to shunt your rear end. Maybe there is some truth in what the driver said about Filipino drivers. They may drive in what appears to be a heart-stopping manner, but they do so with such skill, seizing opportunities to squeeze into gaps with only millimetres to spare. There seem to be relatively few accidents in Manila. Mind you, that is probably because the traffic is moving so slowly, or going nowhere, with horns blaring in frustration. I could never understand why a driver, approaching a stationary line of traffic of infinite length, should imagine that blasting his horn would, like Moses parting the waters of the Red Sea, clear away the hundreds of vehicles blocking the road for miles ahead. Despite the lack of evidence of such miracles, they still do it.

The ubiquitous trikes are Japanese motorbikes with a third wheel to one side, with a little cab built over it. They are the poor man's taxi. The cab is usually big enough to seat two people with luggage behind, but some can seat more. The bike itself will carry the driver and a pillion passenger, or maybe even two on the pillion. I sat in one that carried nine adults and three children. It had a bigger cab than most. As well as the usual forward-facing front seat for two, it had another seat in the front cab facing backwards. Three adults and three children had squeezed in there. The cab also had a rear compartment that could accommodate four. The driver and another adult on the pillion made a total of twelve people on that trike.

Trike - the poor man's taxi

Filipinos are designed to fit into small spaces. I squeezed in the back compartment beside three attractive Filipinas (Male: Filipino, Female: Filipina). The girls all wore brief shorts. I wondered about the smiles on the faces of the two young ladies opposite me as our knees and thighs interlocked. I was smiling too. As the cab rocked and rolled over the rough roads, knees caressed thighs. I am not sure if every caress was a result of the cab rocking, but the cramped conditions did not detract from my enjoyment of the journey.

Four can squeeze in the back

There are tricycles of the pedal variety too. Small Filipino legs power tricycles often laden with overweight tourists along dirt roads on some of the smaller islands, and among the surge of traffic in Manila.

The two-wheeled motorcycle is a machine of amazing versatility. It is not unusual to see a family of five, a mother and father with three children sandwiched between, on one motorbike. Filipinos are creative when it comes to adapting their motorbikes to carry cargo: mountains of fruit and vegetables, building materials, pigs, crates of chickens. I saw one motorcyclist chugging along with a bull strapped into his sidecar. With a little ingenuity they will carry almost anything. I watched a wee man on a motorbike with six, 24-foot long, 4-inch diameter bamboo poles lashed on to it. The forward end protruded about 10 feet in front of the handlebars and was raised to about decapitating height, the after end was almost scraping the road 10 feet behind. Like a knight of olden times, jousting with a lance, he forced his way into the middle of a dense traffic jam.

Carrying cargo

Jeepneys (derived from Jeep and Hackney Cab) are charming wee buses, unique to the Philippines. Well, charming if you have a warped sense of humour and a lust for adventure. Bald tyres are standard. Wheel nuts? Why bother with five when three is adequate. Developed from the World War 2 jeeps left behind by the Americans, they are everywhere, often packed with a ridiculous number of people. How many people can they carry? There is always room for one more! They even sit on the roof and hang on to the rear of the vehicle. Painted in vivid colours, they are often customised with radiator grills in the style of a Rolls Royce, Mercedes, or Cadillac.

Jeepney

Always room for more!

Manila is a vast, sprawling conurbation of around 15 million people, polluted with exhaust fumes. Wearing masks, or holding cloths over their mouths and noses, was commonplace here long before the covid pandemic. The pavements are so cracked and uneven it often looks as if there had been a recent earthquake, which is always a possibility. Street lights are few, drains emit foul smells, and so too does the murky, sick-looking river that runs through the city carrying rafts of floating rubbish. Colourful, dirty, it has a peculiar vibrancy about it. I would hate to live there, but I admit to a fascination with it. I would love to spend more time to try to capture the essence of life in this intriguing city on camera.

Poverty is endemic. Some families were reported in the press to be living on as little as 10 pesos per day (about UK £0.15 or 19 cents US). Rates of pay are low. A waitress told me she earned 200 pesos (UK£3, US$3.80) for a 10-hour shift. With such low rates of pay, it is no surprise that millions of Filipinos seek work abroad as housemaids, nannies, seamen, nurses, carers, and cleaners. In all these jobs they can earn better rates of pay and send money home to support their families.

Life in Manila slums

Elegant high-rise apartments, office blocks, and hotels sit cheek by jowl with crumbling slums and shanty dwellings crawling with people. I wandered through slum areas taking photos of living conditions that astonished me. People bathed from barrels of rainwater on the pavements and in over-crowded alleyways. Give them credit, they are fastidious about their personal cleanliness. Others did their laundry sitting on the ground confronted by huge basins of soapy water and mountains of family clothing. The laundry was hung to dry on lines strung above the narrow alleyways. A man and his wife lived in a ramshackle hut constructed on the pavement. Made of corrugated iron, bits of wood and plastic, it was just big enough to cover a double bed. The roof was not nailed down, but tied and weighted down with old tyres and broken bits of concrete. The street was his workshop, where he sat and repaired broken umbrellas. Their kitchen was a rough wooden shelf nailed on to the outside of their home with a bucket of charcoal on the pavement for cooking.

At least they had a home. The number of people sleeping on the streets, a sheet of cardboard to lie on their only luxury, is one of the saddest sights. With the dust and grime of the city ingrained in their skins, families slept under bridges, in doorways, or out in the open. Haggard mothers sat cross-legged, with a begging bowl, while babies sucked on sagging breasts for whatever meagre nourishment they could provide. It is not uncommon to see babies, not yet able to crawl, left to sleep on a dirty sheet of cardboard, flies crawling over their malnourished bodies, while their mothers forage in rubbish bins for discarded scraps of food.

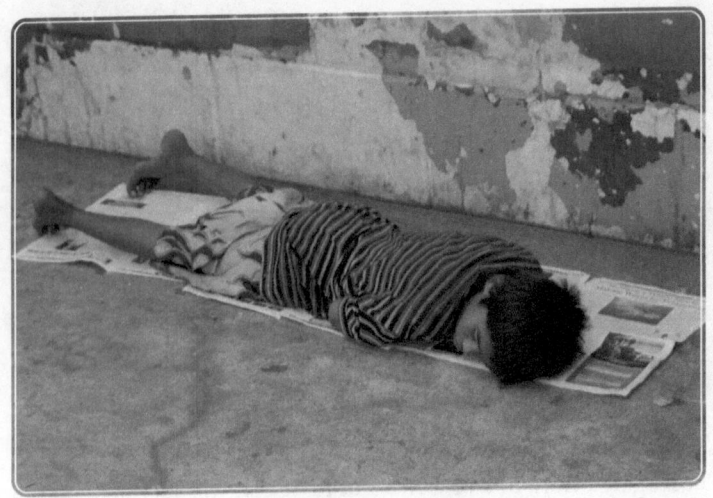

Sleeping on the streets

On my first night there, I took a stroll along the street after dinner. Every bank, hotel, restaurant, and shop seemed to be protected by uniformed security men with revolvers in holsters strapped to their waist. It is an incredibly boring job, standing there all day, or all night, and the rare diversion of a kilted Scotsman walking past - they don't get many of them here - was enough to elicit smiles and greetings. All the gun-toting security guards spoke to me.

"Good evening sir, where are you from?" Not that telling them was enlightening. Few Filipinos have heard of Scotland. Okay, try the UK? No. Great Britain?

"Ah yes, that is in Australia!"

"No, Australia is on the opposite side of the world from Scotland. Ever heard of England?" Vague look. I try to help. "You are speaking English. Which country does that language come from?"

Big smile: "America." This is going to be a long night. Try again.

"Ever heard of Johnnie Walker?" The eyes light up.

"Ah, Johnnie Walker whisky. Very good!"

"Aye, well, that is made in Scotland. That's where I come from." And that was as near as I got to educating them about Scotland. Some words you can say in almost any language and be understood: "Johnnie Walker, Coca Cola, McDonalds, Sexy."

Travelling in the Philippines is never anything less than fascinating. Some buses are comfortable with air-conditioning; others should have been condemned to the scrap heap years ago. A few pesos takes you a long way by bus in the Philippines. And they carry a lot more than people. I once found myself on a provincial bus with a goat standing in the aisle beside me, a hog-tied young pig lying on the floor, a crate of chickens on the seat opposite, and bundles of fruit and vegetables heaped in the aisle, to be climbed over when I had to get out. Anything goes.

A more comfortable alternative is 'the van,' an air-conditioned minibus with no timetable to adhere to. It waits at the terminus until it fills up, or nearly so, and then heads off towards a destination a few hours drive away, picking up more passengers at villages along the route. An air-conditioned minibus may sound luxurious compared with some of the buses you see, but wait. It may start feeling comfortable, but these drivers make their money by carrying passengers, right? That means the more passengers they carry, the more money they make, right? And that means cramming as many people as possible into the minibus, ignoring considerations of health and safety, as well as passenger comfort. You pay to be transported, not to expect the luxury of a seat to yourself.

I shared the front seat with the driver and one other passenger, but I could only gaze in wonder at each stop when yet more people piled in on top of the bodies that were already in the back. On the plus side, that may be a good way to get some introductions. Imagine having an attractive Filipina sitting on your lap for a two or three hour journey. Maybe next time I should go for a seat in the back. They are a gregarious lot and don't seem to have any concept of personal space, but this was incredible; they were writhing about like maggots in there - and nobody seemed to mind. It was more expensive than the bus, but worth every peso for the entertainment value.

Driving along in the provinces is an endless source of wonder. Maniacal bus drivers, forever blasting their horns, threaten to bulldoze anything travelling in the same direction out of the way, and seem intent on mounting an attack on anything coming in the opposite direction while overtaking. He who dares wins! It looks suicidal, but as Lord Nelson once said, "To be daring offers the least risk."

A bus ride offers an endless pastiche of people and places. Every village seems to have a tiny store attached to almost every house, all selling the same wares. I am baffled by the economics of this. If they all sell the same things, who needs to buy? Yet the optimistic ladies sit there all day with an untroubled look on their faces. Men sit in the shade in groups, talk, gamble with cards, and smoke. Nobody seems to do much work.

But this is the middle of the day, when it is daft to work under a scorching sun. The evidence that work has been done earlier is there in the tarpaulins spread out on the roadside covered with rice drying in the sun; crates of vegetables and fruit, harvested in the early morning, waiting for transport to the markets; piles of coconuts awaiting a cooler hour of the day to be husked and the flesh dried as copra for making coconut oil.

Chickens and swine, of many colours and configurations, meander in their search for food among children who are often stark naked, playing in the drainage ditches, or having a pee as nature intended, wherever they happen to be at the time. The men do the same. Even in the cities they will stop on a busy street and pee against a wall. The smell of stale urine is one of the many characteristic aromas in the cities.

In the cool of the morning, women will sit in a ditch washing clothes. Despite the poverty and lack of plumbing, their clothes are clean and they change regularly. Dogs, scrawny and mangy looking, whose pedigree defies description, fornicate with gay abandon, producing yet more complex-looking mongrel pups. The people often do the same; young mothers in their teens are often seen suckling babies instead of attending school. They are never happier than when they have a baby in their arms. The sad part is that the fathers often abandon the girls when they get pregnant, forcing many to migrate to the cities, or abroad, to work for a pittance in factories, hotels, restaurants, and bars, or go into prostitution to earn enough money to support their children. The men find another girl to impregnate. Babies are often left with grandmothers who seem content to have yet another baby to love, and so the cycle of exploitation goes on. An unmarried waitress, pregnant for the second time, shrugged and told me, "It is the way in the Philippines."

Everywhere, the streets are a hive of commerce. And I mean *on* the streets, not just in the shops and offices. Fruit sellers set up their barrow or stalls, caterers cook skewers of chicken and pork on barbecues on wheels, others fry burgers, or sugar coated bananas.

Some sell second hand clothing and shoes, repair watches. Flower sellers set up stalls outside funeral parlours - where better to secure a good trade? Candle sellers were a feature outside churches. The Catholic custom of lighting candles while praying for someone ensures thriving business for candle makers and vendors.

Whatever service society requires, it seems to be available on the streets. And the opportunists are never far away with a good money-saving deal for you: renting a car, a motorbike, a room, diving, tours of the city or island's highlights, which restaurants to go to, a massage, souvenirs, a girlfriend. The taxi driver, hotel receptionist, shop assistant, man in the street, they all know someone who can provide what you want. It can be annoying, but it is understandable given their low incomes.

A refusal does not deter them, and they will ask all sorts of personal questions. "Are you married? Family? Living alone?" (Unheard of in the Philippines where they pack in like sardines and often sleep 3 or 4 to a bed, with more on the floor). They are incredulous. "You live alone? No, that it is not good. You should have a woman to look after you. My cousin/sister/aunty will take good care of you." And off they go again, trying to arrange a meeting, and get you to part with a tip.

Marrying a foreigner, or at least having one for a boyfriend, is the dream of many Filipinas. It is synonymous with financial security, not only for her, but also for her family. The term *boy*friend, is pretty flexible. Talking to a twenty year-old waitress, I learned that she had no time for younger men. They could not be trusted and were always playing around with other girls, she told me. An older man was more likely to be faithful. How old? Well, she had ended a three-year relationship with an Australian in his fifties, who, in spite of her devotion to him, was "messing about with other chicks." He was too young and immature for her. She was now hoping to meet a loving, caring boyfriend in his sixties who would be faithful to her.

The physical beauty and inherent charm of the Filipina is a marketable commodity, and those with foreign boyfriends or husbands enjoy a lifestyle superior to that they could expect with most Filipinos. The fact that their male escorts may be of less than average looks and physique doesn't seem to matter, nor does age. Maturity is synonymous with security - and that is something to treasure in the Philippines where life is affected by so many uncertainties.

CHAPTER 32

Island Hopping

Camiguin, an island lying to the north of its large southern neighbour, Mindanao, claims to have more volcanoes per square kilometre than any other place on earth. Over a hundred years ago during a major eruption, a lava flow buried villages and killed hundreds of people. As if that wasn't bad enough, at the same time an earthquake (catastrophes often come in twos and threes here) caused part of the island to sink below the sea - the part with a cemetery on it. It is a bizarre experience to encounter an entire cemetery underwater when diving.

Being the only customer staying at the small dive resort meant that the waitresses in the restaurant had plenty of time to satisfy their curiosity about me. Travelling alone seemed alien to them.

"Why do you not have a wife or girl friend?"

"I'm too old."

"You are never too old."

"I don't know how to speak Tagalog."

"We'll teach you."

And that was how I leaned my first words of Tagalog, how to compliment a lady, and fix up a date.

I hired a motorbike for a couple of days to explore the island. Driving up a rough, rocky track to a waterfall, the people who lived in the forest were amicable, calling out, "Hello, my friend," as I passed their houses. I bounced my way over the boulders on what they dare to call a road - it was more like a dried-up riverbed. Which it was, for when the tropical rains fall here the mountain roads often become rivers. The houses, built on stilts and made of woven leaves tied to bamboo frames with thatch on the roof, are not much bigger than a garden shed. They cook outside on a fire and take their water from the streams. Children coming home from school walked up several miles of this rough track to their homes in the mountains. They all called out too, and waved to me. Here was the legendary friendliness of the Philippines at its simple, innocent best.

Camiguin jungle house

Bohol is a large island in the central Philippines. I flew into Tagbilaran, a city of about 100,000 people, a shambles of narrow streets with ramshackle stores and crazy traffic - is there any other kind here? The rest of the island is rural in character with cottage industries, rice farming, and fishing along the coasts.

They are very proud of the Chocolate Hills on Bohol, a 'must see' for visitors, the eighth wonder of the world, they say. Conical hills, ranging from about 100 feet to almost 400 feet in height, they have been created by a combination of the dissolution of limestone by rainfall and erosion by rivers after they had been uplifted above sea level and fractured by tectonic processes. Consisting of marine limestone rubble, they contain an abundance of fossils. It is the light of the setting sun that endows them with a chocolate-coloured appearance, hence the name. A unique and intriguing curiosity they are, but to describe them as the eighth wonder of the world is stretching it a bit, in my opinion. Mind you, the Filipino tourist brochures claim to have at least three eighth wonders of the world: the remarkable rice terraces at Banuae (which really are a source of wonder), and the underground river in Palawan are similarly described by enthusiastic promoters of tourism.

Chocolate Hills

It was the white sands and the colourful diving sites of Panglao, a small island connected by bridge to Bohol and only half an hour's taxi ride from the airport, that was the primary attraction for me. The airport has since been relocated to Panglao island.

Panglao Island

I had booked into a pleasant resort on the shore with its own restaurant. Most of the guests were couples, so again I was endowed with some curiosity value in being solo - or maybe it was the kilt that aroused so much interest. Whatever the reason, the room-maids, the waitresses, the boys who tended the gardens, and the security guards all wanted to stop and chat. However, when the spoons came out to join the band that played in the restaurant each evening, that rocketed me up the popularity ratings. Guests dug out cameras to take photographs, the receptionist abandoned the front desk, and the kitchen staff bailed out to come through to the restaurant to listen. Waiters and waitresses smiled, and danced among the tables as they served.

Mehmet and Kim, a Canadian couple, showed a lot of interest and enjoyment while I was playing and invited me to join them at their table afterwards, an invitation they repeated every night after that. Travelling solo does not mean you are always on your own. It is the best way to travel if you want to make friends - and if you are wearing a kilt, you can hardly fail.

Malapascua, to the north of Cebu Island, is a wee island of palm trees and white beaches with around a thousand inhabitants, but its main attraction eluded me: the thresher sharks, which have an upper tail fin as long as their body. Shy creatures (most sharks are), that feed in the depths at night, they come up to a shelf at about 20 metres at dawn to be cleaned by the cleaner wrasse, fish which feed on the parasites that cling to the shark's skin. Each morning at 6 a.m. I was dropping into the depths to watch this sight, but not once did I see a shark of any description. The annoying thing was that others who dived from the same boat, on the same days, in the same general location, always seemed to see at least one. We were scattered around several so-called cleaning stations where the sharks have their morning ablutions performed by the cleaner wrasse, but when they did appear it was never at the one where I lay in wait. Otherwise, the diving at Malapascua was pleasant with some colourful corals and a Japanese patrol boat wreck, and on my last night I offered to take my dive guide and the boat crew out for a drink.

"Where is the best place to go?" I asked in my innocence. My guide smiled.

"Karaoke Bar - it is the *only* place to go."

That was my introduction to Malapascua nightlife: sitting in a rough wooden shack, about 4 metres square with an earth floor, drinking bottles of beer and slaughtering songs in true Filipino fashion. The locals seemed to be enjoying themselves, and after a couple of beers so did I. The more you drink, the better it sounds!

Boracay is the premier holiday destination in the Philippines and has one of the most idyllic beaches in the world: a four-mile sweep of white sand fringed with coconut palms. Washed by the sea, which sparkles in the almost ever-present sunlight, this white crescent of sand is sprinkled with dozens of boats, taking tourists out for a sail. It presents a dazzling scene, bustling with activity.

Boracay Beach

The boats are nearly all traditional outriggers. Some are powered by sail and are very fast, their sleek hulls slicing through the water like a knife. Others, powered by growling, smoking diesel engines, ferry passengers to and from the airport at Caticlan, on the large island of Panay, or carry scuba divers or snorkelers to the dive sites around the island.

There are some good dive sites around Boracay: Crocodile Island is rich with corals: Yapak, spectacular and deep, has a powerful current sweeping up from the depths and over the reef so that it feels like you are clinging on in a gale. Most other sites are middling, but I found Boracay to be the most expensive place to dive in the Philippines.

Every day, a team of professional sandcastle builders create the most amazing sandcastles, and tourists have their photos taken beside them for a fee. Swimmers and sunbathers proliferate daily on the beach and, to ease away the stresses of life, you can lie on a mat on the sand, or in one of the beach-side parlours, and have a relaxing massage, a pleasant way to spend an hour.

Sandcastles are built every day

A team of masseuses worked at a resort with a good restaurant, where I dined in the evenings. They often doubled as waitresses and were always ready to chat with me at my table, complimenting me on my blue eyes and fair skin, telling me that I was handsome and had a good body. Impressed by their impeccable judgement of my aesthetic qualities, I had never felt so good about myself. Okay, I know, I know, but massaging my ego as well as my body worked wonders for my morale, and it was impossible not to give them some trade in the massage parlour after that, with a tip, of course.

Boracay sunset

They had become my friends on Boracay, and one of the waitresses invited me to attend her 20th birthday party. The other waitresses, waiters, and the chefs gathered on the beach after closing time. Sitting in a circle on the sand were these young people in their early twenties, with a Scotsman wearing a kilt, who *had* been his twenties, well… a year or two ago. They were respectful, interested in me, and when we parted company around 1 a.m. the goodnights and handshakes were repeated several times. I felt honoured to have been asked to join them.

Having developed a wee bit of a cold towards the end of the week I was unable to go diving for the last couple of days. However, Shiela, one of the waitresses, had a day off and offered to guide me on a tour of her home province, Aklan, on neighbouring Panay, to spend the day visiting a butterfly farm and a coastal conservation area, and to visit her family. I enjoy meeting people away from the tourist places. To get there we used the ferry, the van, and a tricycle. In Kalibo, the main city in this province, the streets are filled with exhaust fumes from the hordes of trikes. Engines roar, horns blow, people and machines mingle in chaotic fashion. It is pandemonium. Yet somehow it all seems to happen without accident.

Shiela's father made bamboo furniture - and babies in his spare time, twelve of them! Well, her mother helped out with that activity.

"How on earth do you manage to cram 14 people into that wee house?' I asked Shiela. She laughed.

"He had to build four houses to accommodate us all as we grew up, but with the older girls now working away from home, he plans to sell two of the houses."

Her mother, now looking after her grandchildren, had the serene look of someone who loves children - just as well, with four girls followed by eight boys, and who knows how many more grandchildren to come.

After a lunch of fish and rice, we visited the butterfly farm and a conservation area of coastal marshland within a mangrove forest. An important breeding ground for fish and mud crabs, this interesting environment was unlike anything in Scotland. Shiela's neighbours were fishermen who seemed pleased by my interest and were happy to pose for me while taking photos of their catch, finger-sized fish, which are tossed into the frying pan and eaten whole. An interesting day trip, it offered insights into how people live in the provinces.

Also on Boracay, were Kim and Mehmet, the charming Canadian couple I'd met at Panglao the week before. They too were teachers, working in Taiwan for a year, and they were now coming to the end of their holiday in the Philippines. We swapped email addresses and have kept in touch ever since.

My flight to Coron, part of Palawan province in the southwest of the Philippines, was on a small plane which landed at an airstrip on the island of Busuanga. Transport into Coron town was by jeepney, a dusty, bumpy ride over provincial roads. Coron town is not on Coron Island, where I was to stay, but on Busuanga. A boat was waiting to ferry me over to the island.

The coastal scenery here is attractive and offers divers a superb wreck site, with Japanese wrecks from World War II. It was in September 1944 that US bombers, launched from aircraft carriers at Leyte on the extreme east of the Philippines, crossed to this most western province to attack a fleet of Japanese supply ships anchored among the small islands to the west of Coron. The planes, sweeping in low around the hills of the neighbouring islands, mounted a surprise low-level attack and achieved such accuracy with their the bombing and torpedoes they often destroyed the ships' bridges and engine rooms, leaving the rest of the hulls intact. That made them ideal for divers to enjoy, decades later.

Visibility is often not good here, and currents can be very strong where the South China Sea forces its way between islands with only narrow channels between them. However, on this occasion my timing coincided with neap tides, so there was less of a current and visibility was good, allowing panoramic views of the ships as we descended. It was my first experience of serious wreck diving: exploring the interiors, the cargo holds, engine rooms, and several deck levels.

Entering the dark void of the cargo holds, the eyes became accustomed to the gloom and dark shapes became recognisable: a bulldozer, bags of cement, rolls of steel mesh for making aircraft runways. The engine rooms, torn apart by the bombs or torpedoes, allowed light to enter and everything could be seen clearly: huge boilers still intact, propeller tubes, tangled and fractured pipework and cabling, steel plate ripped apart, ladders and girders twisted by the searing heat of explosion; all testifying to the destructive effect of high explosive. I wondered what kind of hell the men who crewed these ships had gone through in that sudden onslaught of explosion and fire. Such intimacy with the devastation caused by the bombing of a ship left a deep impression. This was more than a dive: it was a lesson in history and the folly of man's wanton lust for power.

It was also a lesson on the power of nature to overcome man-made destruction. These stricken ships are now thriving communities of marine life. Big fish loomed out of the gloomy darkness of the cargo holds; lion fish, festooned with feathery spines, danced in the shadows of the wheelhouse. An octopus backed itself into a dark cavity near the stern. A large cuttlefish gazed at us through dopey eyes, with little concern over our presence. Wreck diving is fascinating.

This is very much a frontier area and no one knows how many people live in its remote jungles. There are still indigenous tribes on Palawan and Coron who are shy of outsiders, even other Filipinos, and disappear into the bush if strangers approach. I saw a couple of remote settlements from the dive boat. Living as their ancestors have done for hundreds of years, these tribes inhabit remote coastal bays and jungle-clad hills and have little concept of civilisation, as we have the conceit to call it. Among all the people of the Philippines, they were least affected by World War II. For them, the Japanese invasion had negligible effect. If a Japanese patrol boat ever approached a coastal village they would simply melt into the jungle until it had gone. Living in a remote area of dense jungle with no towns or cities, no natural harbours, factories, or transport routes - nothing of interest to an invading force - these people lived as they had always done, while the 'civilised' world tore itself apart with bombs and terror.

The town of Coron, unsophisticated, with crude homes built on stilts out over the murky waters of the harbour, is a place for fishermen to spend their money in the multitude of karaoke bars that line the jetty. Side by side, each one belting out tortured songs at full volume, all are equally terrible to listen to in a hideous cacophony of noise that bears little resemblance to music. But they love it, and do it every night. It had the kind of inelegant lack of charm that amuses me - for a short time.

Coron pier houses

On my last day on Coron, I sat on the external stairway chatting with the girls who cleaned the rooms as they rested between spells of work. Brown skin, black hair, brown eyes are standard in the Philippines, so my fair skin, blue eyes, and fair hair attracted comment. It was enchanting to have these girls looking into my blue eyes, stroking my fair hair, and telling me, "You are so handsome, Sir John, much better looking than the Filipino men."

And do you know, I was told this so often I even began to believe it!

Coron resort

I had been ambivalent about my first visit to the Philippines. I had hoped it would live up to its reputation for friendliness and excellent diving, and I was not disappointed. With English being one of the official languages of state, communication was not a problem, and its 7,000 islands had plenty of variety to offer in diving and touring. Accommodation and transport are relatively cheap for the budget-conscious traveller, and as well as its own attractions, the Philippines was conveniently situated to become a base from which I could explore other parts of South East Asia.

Thailand, Indonesia, Borneo, Cambodia, Laos,Vietnam, the islands of Micronesia, and the Maldives are all within easy reach and offer some fascinating places to visit, as well as some of the best diving in the world.

This complex country of contrasts possessed a magnetism that was to lure me back again and again.

The End